Loch Ness has a dark and brooding look even in fine weather, due in part to the gloomy coniferous forest that blankets its eastern side, and its great depth, which reaches 700 feet in places. This sombre appearance has undoubtedly had something to do with the growth of the belief that a monster lives in Loch Ness, though it seems that monsters are not unusual in the Great Glen, for another legendary monster also inhabits Loch Oich.

Though the monster has reached its greatest fame in our time, thanks to the efforts of the mass media, it has been known for centuries. It was already something of a celebrity in the days of St Columba, in the sixth century. In a book on the life of the saint there is an account of the beast's being frightened away from an intended victim by the holy man who called on it to go away in God's name. This suggests that Nessie has mellowed over the years; today's monster is supposed to be a shy and peaceful creature, and keeps well away from human beings – which is why he, or she, is so difficult to photograph.

Also in this series in Granada Paperbacks

Welsh Walks and Legends
by Showell Styles
(Illustrated)

West Country Walks and Legends
by J. H. N. Mason
(Illustrated)

Lakeland Walks and Legends
by Brian J. Bailey
(Illustrated)

London Walks and Legends
by Mary Cathcart Borer
(Illustrated)

Scottish Walks and Legends:
The Lowlands and East Scotland
by Janice Anderson and Edmund Swinglehurst
(Illustrated)

Janice Anderson and Edmund Swinglehurst

Scottish Walks and Legends

Western Scotland and the Highlands

A MAYFLOWER BOOK

GRANADA

London Toronto Sydney New York

Published by Granada Publishing Limited in 1982

ISBN 0 583 13443 2

A Granada Paperback Original
Copyright © Janice Anderson and Edmund Swinglehurst 1982

Granada Publishing Limited
Frogmore, St Albans, Herts AL2 2NF
and
36 Golden Square, London W1R 4AH
866 United Nations Plaza, New York, NY 10017, USA
117 York Street, Sydney, NSW 2000, Australia
100 Skyway Avenue, Rexdale, Ontario, M9W 3A6, Canada
61 Beach Road, Auckland, New Zealand

Printed and bound in Great Britain
by Cox and Wyman Ltd, Reading
Set in Plantin

Granada ®
Granada Publishing ®

CONTENTS

ACKNOWLEDGEMENTS

The photographs on pages 18, 89, 99, 180 were supplied by the British Tourist Authority; the one on page 84 by the Scottish Tourist Board. All the other photographs were supplied by Edmund Swinglehurst.

INTRODUCTION

The monsters, giants, mermaids and 'little people' of Scotland figure less in conversation in our age of canned entertainment than once they did, but this does not mean that they have capitulated to the forces of progress and disappeared altogether. Indeed, you have only to talk to anyone who lives by the lochs and in the glens of the Scottish Highlands to discover that the other world of Scotland is still alive and well, though keeping itself to itself.

Express a sympathetic interest in the legendary events and peoples of the Highlands and you will soon be told stories that add an extra dimension to your appreciation of ruined castles, abbeys, mountain-girt lochs, deep and forested glens and all those other places that inspire wonder and delight in visitors to Scotland.

If you know the story of the Massacre in Glen Coe, for instance, you have only to be in Glen Coe on a stormy day, or even on a sunny one with the sun breaking through the glens of the Three Sisters and silhouetting them against its rays, to feel anew the horror of that snowy night in 1692 when a company of Campbells attacked their hosts, the MacDonalds, and killed or drove them out of their valley to die in the mountains. Awareness of the story adds drama to what would otherwise be simply a scenic drive – albeit a magnificent one – and contributes to one's knowledge of the character of the Scottish people.

The stubborn and freedom-loving characteristics which brought about the tragedy of Glen Coe are found in many of the Scottish legends, whether they are embroideries on real events or about mythical beings, and are probably the

7

result of the admixture of peoples who made Scotland and whose cultures the legends represent.

The original inhabitants of Scotland were the Picts, who inhabited the high land called Alban, and the Britons who occupied the southern uplands. The Scots arrived in about AD 250 from Ireland, bringing with them their sacred stone of Destiny. They soon conquered the Picts, and set up their capital in Dalriada, the land now called Perthshire. With them to Scone went the Stone of Destiny on which all their kings were crowned and which today rests under the Coronation Chair in Westminster Abbey. In the meantime, Norsemen had settled on the west coast and the islands, contributing some of their own Nordic culture to the Scottish melting pot.

The Nordic genius for creating epic myth merged easily with pagan beliefs and in a country where even the weather contributes to the evocative environment, it was natural that the supernatural should flourish. Relics of pagan beliefs still survive today, though often the meanings of rituals and customs have long been lost. The story of the 'family' of stones at Ben Lyon is a case in point. The stones are solemnly brought out of their shielding every spring, while an appointed person restores their house after the ravages of winter. There is little doubt that the many stories of the little people, mermaids, sea horses and monsters are pagan in origin.

The clan system also produced its share of fictionalized history, and some of these stories have been included here to demonstrate their legendary qualities. How other than as legend could one classify the story of Maclean of Duart on Mull (p. 169) or the Faery Flag of Dunvegan (p. 81) which prosaic historians will claim to be not a gift to the MacLeods from a faery princess but a standard captured off some Viking ship or brought to Scotland from the Middle East?

As well as the legends, there are endless stories of ghosts

and apparitions current in Scotland, and most people you meet will have their own versions of them. Perhaps the episodes – for they are not really stories in that they often do not have a regular beginning-middle-end shape – will be recounted with a wry smile in case you are an unbeliever, but the fact that they are preserved and told at all says something about the Highlanders' attitude to them.

Legends and fairy stories are, of course, somewhat subjective since they depend for their continued existence very much on being passed on orally. There are two reasons for oral repetition being the best way to keep them alive; firstly, the stories are enlivened and enriched by the talent and experience of the story-teller, and secondly, they are not subjected to the prosaic rationalism that overwhelms some people when they see something in cold print. Legends, like truth, must be free and if that freedom makes them elusive we think this is something to be accepted with delight, for the heart, as Pascal said, has its reasons.

In selecting tales from the vast store of stories and legends known in the Highlands and the North of Scotland, we have tried to include some with which people may be familiar, though they do not know their place of origin, and some, unfamiliar in themselves, which are connected with places that are very well known. In this way, we hope to add an extra dimension to a familiar journey, or introduce readers to places they may never have thought of visiting except that the legend has induced them to do so.

The stories have come from many sources. Often, when talking to Scottish people, we would be told stories we had already read in the great collections of Gaelic folk tales. Did the people telling them also know them because they had read them, or heard them on radio and television, or because they were part of the story-telling tradition: tales told at bedtime by mother or round the fire by grandad, and passed down in a family for many generations? It is impossible to establish the source for sure.

Be that as it may, we must, like most other modern writers and editors of Scottish folk tales and legends, acknowledge as our main sources of the stories in this book, the great Victorian collectors of stories in the Gaelic, notably John Francis Campbell of Islay and John Gregorson Campbell of Tiree, whose tradition of sound scholarship has been well upheld in this century by John Lorne Campbell of Barra and Dr Kathleen Briggs.

The bibliography at the end of the book lists those publications which were most helpful, or which we read with the greatest pleasure.

The Walks

Most of the walks included in this book have been planned so that they can be undertaken by people of all ages, though children under six will find some of them too long to do without a piggy-back from a willing dad or friend, or perhaps too hilly to undertake at all. In some cases, the walks are along planned tracks in areas under the authority of the Forestry Commission, or along specified paths such as the West Highland Way; yet others are along unpaved and unfenced minor roads which make perfectly good walkways since there is little traffic along them; others still, take in areas of hill or farmland with no obvious path.

On the walks we have estimated the approximate distance of the round trip, assuming that you are going to end your walk where you began it. The one or two exceptions are clearly indicated. We have not attempted to be exact because there are often slight alternatives to the path suggested. Nor have we given estimated times for the walks because this will vary from person to person, and according to how often you will want to stop to look at things.

Roughly speaking, you should be able to walk at four miles an hour without too much effort over relatively level ground. For hill walking, the rate may be two to two-and-a-half miles an hour.

The word 'tracks' needs some explanation. On the Ordnance Survey maps there are ways marked by broken lines which in some cases are fenced but paved roads, and in others open unpaved tracks across a field indicated only by the fact that farm or forestry vehicles use them. In some cases, we have called them 'tracks' to be distinguished from 'paths' by the fact that a track, as we call it, has seemed to us capable of allowing passage for vehicles. In some cases these tracks may simply be access routes across private land.

The map references given for each walk are based on the Ordnance Survey 1:50,000 series and pin-point the starting place.

Walking in Scotland

The footpath system which is such a feature of walks in England hardly exists in Scotland. Broadly speaking, you will either be walking along single-track minor roads or across private land. In many cases, the land is open moorland covered in grass or heather and very inviting for exploratory walks to the tops of hills.

Farmers and landowners do not, on the whole, mind your walking over their land as long as you treat it with the proper respect. Where you have to enter their land near a farm building it is courteous to ask permission to do so. We have never encountered any refusals, but the continued goodwill of those who own and work the land will depend on the behaviour of those who walk over it. Please therefore always make sure that you do not do any damage to fences, that you close gates and that you do not frighten sheep, cattle or other animals that may be within the fenced-in areas. This is particularly important in springtime during the lambing season.

One other note of warning: during the shooting and stalking season certain walks can be dangerous. Inform yourself locally about whether a shoot or stalk is taking place, and avoid the area.

If you enjoy something more than a short stroll around the place where the legend is set, you may be tempted to take off across hillsides to the ever-beckoning horizon. If you do – and this is particularly important on mountain sides cut by steep ravines – remember that the weather in Scotland can change very rapidly. You can be surrounded by thick mist or rain, and in springtime even get caught in a snowstorm, with devastating speed. Always carry a map and compass with you and learn how to use them before you set off, and listen to local weather forecasts before you set off in the morning. If you also carry a whistle, and some food, you should be all right on all the walks here *providing your clothing is sensible* – and this is vital. Never go wandering in the countryside in Scotland in thin clothes and town sandals. You should always carry a sweater and a water-proof anorak or jacket however hot the day when you start out, and always wear reasonably stout shoes, with ridged soles: smooth leather or plastic soles slip on grassy hillsides.

Wherever you walk in northern Scotland, remember the summer mountain code – it could save your life.

Before you go:
Learn the use of map and compass
Know the weather signs and local forecast
Plan within your capabilities
Know simple first aid and the symptoms of exposure
Know the mountain distress signals
Know the country code

When you go:
Never go alone
Take windproofs, woollens and survival bag

Travelling round Scotland

We have assumed that you will probably be driving and therefore our walks start near a place where you may park your car. If you are not travelling by car, you will find that there is a bus service going somewhere near the start of most of the walks, but these services may be only once a day in each direction, so we have decided not to include specific route numbers. Bus timetables can be obtained from the Scottish National Tourist Office in Edinburgh and from most local tourist offices, where staff can usually advise you on the frequency of services.

The Scottish National Tourist Board's information centres are also very helpful in telling you about what's on in their locality. The National Trust for Scotland also has excellent information centres at sites owned by them.

In writing this book and its counterpart *Southern Scotland and the Lowlands* we have travelled far and wide over Scotland and have discovered many beautiful places that we had not visited before as well as more fascinating facts about the places that we already knew.

The result of our research has confirmed in us more than ever the conviction that Scotland has a beauty that never fails to surprise and enthral and a mystery that bewitches those who take time to be more than just summer tourists.

Wherever we have been we have been met with courtesy and have discovered something of interest, and we have rarely come across that dourness for which the Scots are supposedly reputed.

The accommodation, whether in an old baronial manor or at a humble bed and breakfast establishment, has been exemplary and the elbow grease supplied by Scottish landladies absolutely dazzling.

A

THE FAR NORTH

The Seal Hunter of Duncansby Head
The Red Priest of Strathnaver
Bonnie Prince Charlie's Gold
The Ironsmiths of Ben Loyal
Lord Reay Beats the Devil
The Devil and MacLeod of Assynt

1. THE SEAL HUNTER OF DUNCANSBY HEAD
John O'Groat's

John O'Groat's is not quite the most northern point of mainland Britain, an honour which goes to Dunnet Head near Thurso, but most people think of it as such. The coast around this part of Scotland is wild and rocky and there are splendid views across the Pentland Firth to the Orkneys. The village of John O'Groat's is said to have been founded in the early sixteenth century by a Dutchman, John de Groot, who designed an octagonal table in an octagonal room in a house with eight entrances in order to eliminate quarrels about precedence among his brothers. There is a flagpole down by a hotel on the sea's edge which is supposed to mark the site of the de Groot house.

Because of its position, John O'Groat's, which otherwise is not an attractive village, receives many visitors from all over Britain in summer and plenty of good facilities have been built for them, including camping grounds and caravan parks.

Away from the village, the beach is attractive, while sea birds and seals can be seen off Duncansby Head, two miles to the east of John O'Groat's. This is an area of exciting cliff scenery, natural sea·chasms and the seal colonies which have given rise to an ancient legend about a seal hunter who lived in this remote part of Scotland.

According to the story, the seal hunter was a poor man who had to work very hard hunting seals in order to make enough money to keep his family. Whatever the weather, the seal hunter would go out scrambling along the treacherous rocks looking for seals. Killing them was not easy, for they were very wary of hunters and he would sometimes have to lie in wait for hours hoping that he

17

Duncansby Head.

would be able to get close enough to the seals to jump out on them and knife one of them before they slipped away into the sea.

One day, the fisherman caught sight of a particularly fine specimen and he determined to kill it, for its flesh would feed his family and its pelt would fetch a good price in the marketplace.

For several hours, the hunter made a very cautious approach until finally he came within reach of the seal. Waiting for a moment when the magnificent animal was distracted, he leapt up from behind a rock and drove his knife into the seal's neck.

He was about to draw the knife and plunge it in again when he slipped on some seaweed. Before he could recover his balance the seal had slid away into the water and disappeared, leaving a faint trace of blood on the rocks on which it had been sitting.

Sadly, because he had lost the seal and his knife, the seal hunter returned to his boat and rowed away from the rocks towards the beach where he kept his craft in a cave above high water mark. Having secured it, he walked up the cliff path towards his home. He had not walked very far when he heard a horseman coming up behind him at a gallop. Wondering why the man was in such a hurry, the hunter stopped and looked back. The horseman drew level and nodded to him to climb on the horse. The seal hunter was about to refuse this lift from a stranger but his fatigue and his depression at the unsuccessful day's hunting made him eager to get home so he climbed up behind the horseman.

To his surprise and consternation, the horse set off at a gallop in the direction from which he had just come. Reaching the top of the cliff at Duncansby Head, it leapt into the air and the seal hunter found himself spinning down towards the sea and then through the water.

Down and down he went, thinking that his end had surely come when, suddenly, he landed gently on the sea-bed in a rocky amphitheatre in the centre of which lay a large seal on a rock surrounded by attendant seals. As he arrived, the surrounding seals drew back, leaving an avenue for him to walk through. As he did so, he realized with an icy shiver of guilty fear that the large seal on the rock was the one that he had stabbed.

Had he been able to do so, the seal hunter would have run away but there was nowhere for him to go. As he walked forward, the seals closed in around him until he had arrived at the side of their wounded companion.

With gestures of their flippers, the seals motioned him to remove the knife from the seal's neck while the great seal itself, evidently their king, to judge by the deference the other seals showed, looked steadily at the hunter with his large, sad eyes.

The hunter took hold of the handle of the dagger he had lost only a few hours earlier and felt a terrible sadness that he should have to kill these creatures so that his own family might survive. Filled with remorse at his actions, he stroked the seal's wounded neck as he withdrew the knife and to his astonishment he saw that as the knife slid out of the wound the torn flesh came together as if it had never been cut. When he had withdrawn the whole blade the seal sat up and looked at him gratefully and the other seals crowded round and patted him with their flippers. The seal hunter could hardly believe that this was happening to him, nor could he comprehend the extraordinary fact that he was able to communicate with the seals without talking to them. In the time that he had been on the sea-bed with them, he had learnt a great deal about their lives and their society, almost as much, in fact, as he knew about the community in which he lived. This knowledge, he realized, would make it impossible for him ever to kill a seal again and later, as he rode once more on the back of the stranger's horse to his village, he wondered how he would make his living.

The legend does not provide the answer.

THE WALKS:

1. FROM JOHN O'GROAT'S VILLAGE TO DUNCANSBY HEAD.
2. FROM JOHN O'GROAT'S TO DUNCANSBY NESS.

MAP SQUARE:

Ordnance Survey Sheet 7/380726
Two pleasant easy headland walks.

John O'Groat's is on the A9, the Great North Road, which follows the east coast up from Inverness. The A836, which branches off the A9 at Bonar Bridge, offers another route to John O'Groat's through the centre of Sutherland to Tongue and then along the north coast via Thurso. The railway line from Inverness runs north along the coast as far as Helmsdale and then turns inland, dividing into the Wick and Thurso lines at Halkirk. Several bus routes also serve John

O'Groat's. Along the coast, services 22 and 201 go to Wick and then on by Dunnets Motors to John O'Groat's. From Wick, service 80 goes along the coast to John O'Groat's.

The walks suggested for the John O'Groat's countryside both start in the village. The FIRST SUGGESTED WALK is along the minor road which runs due east from the village to Duncansby Head, just over a mile and a half away. The walk is easy, and goes gently downhill until it reaches the Head, where it rises to the edge of the cliffs. The headland is 210 feet high and among the most beautiful in northern Scotland. From this vantage point some of the finest cliff views in Britain can be enjoyed, looking across the South Ronaldsay, Stroma and the Orkneys. A mile to the south the huge Stacks of Duncansby stand isolated from the shoreline. On the headland itself are the lighthouse, coastguard station, and an underground chamber built for the Royal Observer Corps.

The SECOND SUGGESTED WALK, also starting in the village, follows the track leading off to the left about halfway along the minor road to Duncansby Head. This leads to Duncansby Ness, another fine viewpoint looking due north. This track is parallel to, but half a mile away from, the A9 which comes to an end at the land's end, where there is a hotel, camping site and caravan park. The pier here is a good viewpoint.

2. THE RED PRIEST OF STRATHNAVER
Strathnaver

The River Naver runs from Loch Naver in the centre of Sutherland to the north and meets the Atlantic at the village of Bettyhill. It flows through a green and beautiful valley, inhabited from earliest times, as the cairns along the roadside indicate. By one of these cairns at Skail Corner, so legend has it, is buried Maol Ruadh, the 'red priest', a follower of St Columba who lived in the seventh century. At Skail is a small ruined house which is said to have been his home, and not far from the house are the cairns marking an ancient burial area where Maol Ruadh is said to be buried.

According to local tradition, Maol Ruadh prophesied that Strathnaver would be depopulated and repopulated when his bones were washed out to sea. Those who believe that fact can often be stranger than fiction think that the first part of this prophecy came true during the misguided attempts by the nineteenth-century Duke of Sutherland to improve the profitability of his northern Scottish estates by turning the land over to sheep grazing. This meant that the crofters who scraped a meagre living out of the reluctant land had to be moved out of the way to the sea coast or encouraged to emigrate to seek their fortunes, in Canada and other colonies.

The Clearances, as this tragic period in the history of the Highlands is called, though a historical reality have become almost legendary and tales of oppression and victimization by the Duke of Sutherland's men are legion. The Duke employed two men, Patrick Sellar and William Young, to make a study of the Sutherland estate to discover how best to improve its productivity and profitability. About this, there were two viewpoints. One held that the people of

22

Strathnaver.

Sutherland were 'torpid with idleness and most wretched', and living in hovels; another spoke of farms with milk cows and fields with barley and oats. At any rate the Duke, formerly the Marquess of Stafford before marrying Elizabeth, Countess of Sutherland in her own right, thought that the land could be improved and gave his lieutenants *carte blanche* to go ahead and move the peasants out of the area intended for sheep raising.

Most of the people who lived in Strathnaver were Mackays and the land here had been their home for generations. They had no wish to leave their native soil and when the Duke's men arrived to order them to depart they resisted. The answer of the Duke's men was to burn down their homes. The despair and suffering that resulted from these high-handed methods left a legacy of stories that have blackened the name of the well-meaning Duke ever since.

Historians point out that the Sutherlands did some good on their lands, the Duke building hundreds of miles of roads and erecting many bridges in Sutherland, and the Duchess supplying bedding and clothes to many of those in need, but in the main public opinion was against them.

In 1815, petitions alleging acts of cruelty, injury and oppression by Sellar were brought before the Sheriff of Sutherland and examined in the Court of Judiciary in Edinburgh. Sellar was found innocent, much to the disgust of those people who had suffered at his hands. Particularly incensed was one Donald MacLeod, a stonemason who had been evicted several times. MacLeod attacked the Sutherlands and their lieutenants incessantly and consequently became their victim. They pursued him and his wife and four children, driving them out of every home they set up until finally, while MacLeod was working away from home, they set fire to the house and furniture. The local people had been warned not to offer them shelter, and while Mrs MacLeod was taking her children to the place where her husband was working she became insane from worry and stress. Defeated by this tragic turn of events, MacLeod left the Highlands and settled in Edinburgh – just one among thousands of evicted people in Sutherland.

In accordance with the prophecy of the Red Priest of Strathnaver twelve centuries before, the land began to be repopulated again after a great flood which swept over the saintly man's grave and perhaps swept his bones out to sea.

The repopulation was slight, however, and mostly in the lower reaches of the valley of the River Naver. Today ruined crofts may still be seen scattered across Strathnaver and though new homes have been built, they do not house a thriving population for there is little work and many young people leave for the large urban centres to look for employment.

THE WALK:
FROM DALVINA LODGE, NEAR SYRE, IN STRATHNAVER, SOUTH TO THE NAVER FOREST, ALONG THE NAVER RIVER, AND BACK TO SYRE.

MAP SQUARE:
Ordnance Survey Sheet 10/696440
A 4½ mile walk in the heart of Strathnaver.

The valley of the River Naver is prettier and more gentle in appearance than many of the wild and rugged straths of northern Scotland. Its hills slope gently away from the river, with frequent green fields in which sheep graze, and many well-cared-for cottages. The road through Strathnaver is the B873, a mainly single-track road with passing places, which turns off the A836 at Altnaharra, twenty miles north of Lairg.

Syre, the village by Dalvina Lodge, the start of our walk, is very neat with attractive houses, and is dominated by the white-painted, red-roofed corrugated-iron church, with its neat churchyard on the opposite side of the road, and by elegant Syre House on its grassy knoll, which is thick with daffodils in springtime.

Dalvina Lodge lies over the river from Syre. You enter the Forestry Commission's Naver Forest land by the gate opposite Dalvina Lodge. From here, you walk along the road used by the Commission's work vehicles. This is a comparatively easy stroll across low scrubland, though the road is unpaved. After three-quartes of a mile you will come to the forest plantation proper, marked by a boundary fence.

The road continues ahead through the fence here, but the forest is also fenced along the river bank and as you cannot – or should not – climb the fence, you must turn right here, away from the road. You will see a step-ladder over the fence on to the river bank.

Climb over this and continue walking south along the path which walkers before you have trodden in the heather. This path offers a delightful walk, the serried ranks of conifers on your left hand, and the shallow waters of the Naver on your right, with the B873 following its far bank.

After approximately a mile and a half you will see ahead of you an island in the river. A wooden and steel-rope suspension bridge takes you on to the island, with another one on the other side of the island to take you on to the river's western bank. Here, you can join the B873, turning north again to walk back to Syre, thus completing this circular walk in the heart of Strathnaver.

3. BONNIE PRINCE CHARLIE'S GOLD
Tongue

In the very north of Sutherland, right on the northern coast of mainland Britain, is the beautiful sea loch known as the Kyle of Tongue. The eight-mile-long loch has steep sides and towering above its southern shore are the spectacular slopes of Ben Hope and Ben Loyal. On the eastern side of the loch is the village of Tongue, an attractive place with stone houses and several good hotels. Below the village lies the modern causeway which carries the A838 across the Kyle.

At the time of the '45 rising the loch was navigable all the way up the valley between the mountains of Ben Loyal and Ben Hope. This was the sheltered water into which the former naval sloop HMS *Hazard* nosed its way one spring day in 1746. The *Hazard* had been captured by the Jacobites, who re-christened her the *Prince Charles*. She was presently loaded with supplies and £12,000 in gold for Bonnie Prince Charlie's beleaguered army at Inverness. The ship had come from Dunkirk. Her journey had not been easy: there had been storms, and privateers who had perhaps got wind of the cargo she was carrying had attacked her.

The captain's original intention had been to sail up the Moray Firth to Inverness but no sooner had he entered the gulf than a naval ship that guarded the entrance to Inverness had sailed out to attack him. Since it was more powerful than the *Hazard*, her captain, deciding that discretion was the better part of valour, had fled north, rounding Duncansby Head and heading for the Kyle of Tongue with navy ships still in pursuit. The captain had chosen the Kyle because its waters were shallow and the

English ships with their deeper draught would not be able to follow the *Hazard*.

The *Hazard* sailed into the Kyle of Tongue towards evening. As darkness fell, her captain ordered the unloading of the gold and supplies, hoping that they could be got up the valley and over the hill towards Altnaharra before anyone became aware of the operation.

By daybreak, the men from the *Hazard* were still struggling towards the head of the Kyle with their rich cargo. Word of their slow progress had reached the Mackays, who had never thrown in their lot with Prince Charles. The news brought to them at Castle Varrich of the gold and supplies that watchers at Tongue had seen unloaded from the *Hazard* was incentive enough to send the Mackays chasing after the Jacobite party. A force of them, joined with men from the *Sheerness* which had been following the *Hazard*, were soon in pursuit. Unhampered by the gold and cargo which were slowing down the men from the *Hazard*, the Mackay party moved quickly. Circling Ben Loyal, they soon found themselves looking down the valley up which the Jacobite party was struggling.

The sight of the enemy above them sent a chill of fear and dismay through the Jacobites, already dispirited after their long and weary voyage from France. There was clearly no way out for them but to stand and fight the Mackays' superior forces. They were determined to do everything possible to prevent the gold falling into Mackay hands and, as the Mackays advanced down the valley towards them, they turned off the path in the direction of a lochan, with the intention of jettisoning their valuable load. Some of them managed to reach the lochan before the Mackays attacked but the majority were obliged to turn and fight, still with the gold and the other supplies in their possession. The encounter was brief and not too bloody because, faced by a more numerous and fresher force, the

Jacobite captain quickly surrendered rather than see his men massacred.

The gold and stores were collected up by the victors while the vanquished Jacobites were taken prisoner and marched back down the Kyle to be embarked on the *Sheerness* for transportation to a prison.

This attempt to bring help to Prince Charles' Highland army did not end here, firstly because Prince Charles, desperate for the money to pay his troops, sent a force of 1500 men to try to get the gold back, but they were attacked and captured, and secondly because a legend soon grew up round so romantic an event.

The legend was, of course, a legend of treasure at the bottom of a lochan that lies on the great sweep of heather-covered hills that rise to the heights of Ben Loyal and Ben Hope. The legend speaks of a lochan called 'Haakon' as being the resting place of Prince Charlie's gold – probably tiny Loch Hacoin or Hakel which lies inland from Tongue on what used to be the A838 before the causeway was built. No gold has ever been found, though rumours of people who have come across occasional gold pieces have circulated for years. Like most rumours they are difficult to prove or disprove, and it could be that at least some of Bonnie Prince Charlie's gold still lies at the bottom of Haakon.

THE WALK:
FROM TONGUE TO LOCH
HAKEL, RETURNING TO
TONGUE THE SAME WAY
OR VIA KINLOCH LODGE
AND THE WESTERN
SHORE OF THE KYLE.

MAP SQUARE:
Ordnance Survey Sheet
10/591568
An easy walk in search of
the Prince's gold!

Tongue lies at the junction of the A838 and the A836, two roads which also meet further south near Lairg on Loch Shin.

Tongue: Castle Varrick (Mackay Castle) in the background.

Both roads are good – they are narrow, but passing places are plentiful and easily seen – and provide superb scenery of mountains, moor, forest and coast. People using public transport have only one bus service to Tongue.

Tongue is a good centre for walking and has many paths to offer the visitor. Near the village, overlooking the Kyle, are the remains of Castle Varrich (or Bharraich), a feudal castle which may have been a stronghold of the Norsemen and which was certainly a Mackay stronghold.

Our SUGGESTED WALK in this area is to Lochan Hakel, about two and a half miles from Tongue. Take the road to Ribigill and Kinloch which branches off the A838 hairpin bend by the Tongue Hotel in Tongue, and is sign-posted 'Tongue Village'. This road was, in fact, the main road round the Kyle until the causeway was built. It passes a caravan and camping site and, after about half-a-mile, a footpath to the right which leads to Castle Varrich. Keeping to the 'main' road (which is narrow with passing places) you will cross the Rhian Burn and after about a mile and a quarter *from the start of the walk, pass a turning on the left to Ribigill (which you ignore this time: you will be taking it on our next walk), and then start climbing quite steeply along the edge of An Garbh Chnoc (522 feet). The lochan is another mile and a quarter further on. From here, the view of the 2504-feet Ben Loyal is very fine indeed, its many summits standing out clearly, particularly when they are lit by the late afternoon sun. At the lochan's southern tip and on the road further south are several sites of ancient marked and carved stones – more interesting relics of the past history of this grand countryside than Prince Charlie's mythical gold! To complete the walk, return to Tongue either by the way you have come or by carrying on along the main road past Kinloch Lodge and up the west side of the Kyle, crossing the A838 causeway to get back to Tongue. The latter route is, of course, considerably longer, adding some eight miles to the walk.*

4. THE IRONSMITHS OF BEN LOYAL
Ben Loyal

Ben Hope and Ben Loyal are two splendid mountains in the north of Sutherland. When approached from Altnaharra to the south their heather-clad slopes soar gently to their summits, but on their northern sides they are like the walls of two great fortresses, full of sheer cliffs and canyons which present a forbidding challenge to anyone who approaches them from the sea.

Ben Loyal lies to the east of the Kinloch river which flows into the Kyle of Tongue and on its eastern bank is Loch Loyal past which runs the road to the village of Tongue. Seen from the loch on a clear day, the landscape seems to stretch endlessly in every direction, but in bad weather it is easy to feel that one is in the most isolated place on earth.

It is generally believed that the centre of Ben Loyal is rich in iron ore and that its magnetic field is strong enough to deflect compasses. People on a wavelength with the supernatural believe that inside the mountain there is a whole community of dwarf furnace men and iron-foundry workers who only come out on to the earth's surface at night.

How these little people got down into the bowels of Ben Loyal is told in a legend that harks right back to the Garden of Eden.

It appears that when Adam and Eve were ordered out of the Garden they settled in Scotland, which to all Scotsmen is, of course, the next best thing. Having eaten of the fruit of the Tree of Knowledge, Adam and Eve began to behave like most human beings and in a short while they had many children running around their home. Like most mothers,

Eve found that a family was very nice but also very exhausting and after a few years she became lazy about keeping all her brood washed and in clean clothes all the time.

The condition of Eve's children had not gone unnoticed by passing angels, and it did not take long for stories about the children's ill-kempt and dirty appearance to reach the ears of the Lord. He was a little upset about it as Eve had been an exemplary resident of the Garden of Eden before succumbing to the Serpent's temptation. He, therefore, called up one of His more reliable angels and told him to send a message to Eve warning her that she would soon receive a visit from one of the heavenly angels responsible for looking after the problems of mothers. When Eve received the message about the impending visit she became anxious, for she did not want a bad report to go back to the Lord. On the other hand, she knew from experience that with her large family it was impossible to have them all looking spick and span at once because the first one to be washed and neatly dressed would be in a mess again before she had even got round to cleaning up number ten.

She consulted with Adam who unhelpfully told her that looking after children was a woman's job. No one else could offer any more constructive suggestions so on the day that the Lord's inspector was due to arrive she got up early and took all her children down to the loch by herself. For two hours she scrubbed and washed and buttoned and combed. She seemed to have made little headway when suddenly she heard someone calling her. She knew the voice well and suddenly she was filled with great apprehension for this was no angel who was visiting her, but the Lord Himself.

Desperately Eve looked around her brood and saw that half of them were still unwashed and their clothes were torn and dirty. There was no way in which she could get them cleaned before the Lord arrived. Suddenly she remembered a nearby cave in the side of Ben Loyal. Warning her clean children to sit still and be good, she drove the other ones before her to the cave and hid them deep in its interior.

When she got back to the loch she found that the Lord had been and gone and the children were once more engaged in getting themselves into their usual state of dirt and disarray.

Eve sat down on a rock among the heather, took a deep breath and congratulated herself on having coped with a difficult situation. Now all she had to do was to collect her other children from the cave and go home. When she returned to Ben Loyal, she could not find her children; they had completely disappeared. Although she and Adam spent many long weary days looking for them, they never saw the children again. Adam and Eve were never to know that the little ones had wandered off into the mountain and set up their own community in the heart of the iron-ore belt. There they discovered how to smelt the ore and turn it into metal. They began manufacturing all kinds of objects which they sold to the surface people at night.

Near Loch Loyal there is a stone about which it is said that if you place an iron object on it a replica will be found by its side the following day. So the ironsmiths of Ben Loyal, the lost children of Adam and Eve, are still busy at their work to this day.

THE WALK:	MAP SQUARE:
FROM TONGUE TO THE	Ordnance Survey Sheet
FOOT OF BEN LOYAL, AND	10/591568
BACK TO TONGUE.	A 7 mile walk dominated by Ben Loyal.

Ben Loyal is a deceptive mountain. From the south it appears to rise slowly to a peak of 2400 feet in a great sweeping expanse of heather where in the early days of spring you will see local peat cutters at work piling up their store of winter fuel which has to be dried out during the summer. On these slopes there are herds of deer, raised for commercial exploitation, though you may not catch a glimpse of them for they are difficult to spot against the blue-brown heather.

On its north side, Ben Loyal is quite another mountain. Steep cliffs and canyons plunge towards the valley of the Alt Lon Malmsgaig which runs parallel to the upper part of the Kyle of Tongue and empties into it at the village itself.

The walk from Tongue to the north wall of Ben Loyal is impressive but not difficult. Leave Tongue from the same point as the walk for 'Prince Charlie's Gold', that is at the road to Ribigill and Kinloch marked 'Tongue Village' on the hairpin bend of the A838 where it curves round the village at the Tongue Hotel, a charming shooting-lodge-type establishment. Passing a camping and caravan site you carry on over the Rhian Burn and then take the left fork to Ribigill Farm and follow it south towards Ben Loyal. After half a mile on a metalled road you come to the cluster of farm buildings. At this point the road becomes a track, from where the view of Ben Loyal with its four peaks is very fine. Ignore the right-hand turning into Ribigill Farm and keep to the path as you descend into the valley. About a mile and three quarters south of Ribigill you arrive at Cunside. From here Ben Loyal towers over you and a track past the cottage at Cunside leads up the grassy slopes to the most northerly peak of the Ben Loyal ridge, the 2300-foot Sgor Chaonasaid. We suggest you end your walk at Cunside, however. Those slopes ahead are very steep and the peaks above them are dangerous except for practised climbers.

Tongue Village with Ben Loyal in the distance.

5. LORD REAY BEATS THE DEVIL
Smoo Caves

The north coast of Scotland between Loch Eriboll, christened 'Orrible' by soldiers stationed there during World War II, and the Kyle of Durness is a wild area, with cliffs and gullies cutting into the land. Never does the landscape look a better setting for encounters with the supernatural than when the sea mists glide in between the headlands and familiar features dissolve in the low-lying clouds.

To the east of Eriboll, thought by some to be the most beautiful of Scottish sea lochs, the cliff tops are still littered in many places with the debris of the soldiers' encampments but behind the cliffs lie vast moors rising to 1260 feet at Beinn Ceannabeinne and 1387 feet at Meal Meadhonach.

Below the cliffs stretch vast empty sandy beaches that, if the weather were kinder, would vie with the best in the world. Two miles from Durness are the Smoo Caves.

This extraordinary phenomenon has been formed by the Allt (river) Smoo which reaches the coast at cliff-top level some 100 feet above the sea and then drops straight down a cavern, reappearing again at sea level. The outer cave can be visited but the inner cave system with its stalagmites is not safe. It is, anyway, the outer cave that concerns us here for, according to legend, it was the scene of the final act in a local lord's duel with the devil.

The first Lord Reay, Donald, Chief of Mackay, was a bit of a devil himself as it happens. A swashbuckling soldier, he took a regiment of his clansmen to serve in the army of Gustavus Adolphus whose generalship had altered the course of the Thirty Years War. When the War was finally ended in 1648, Lord Reay, instead of returning to Scotland, travelled around Europe. One night, while carousing in a tavern with a friendly stranger, he learned that his drinking companion was none other than the devil himself. 'The devil you are,' Lord Reay exclaimed and, instead of showing a proper fear, proceeded to try to extract from his friend some of the secrets of his power over men. The devil was not prepared to give up his secrets just for the asking, however, and he suggested instead that if Lord Reay were really sincere about becoming practised in the art of devilry he should join the devil's school at Padua in Italy.

Lord Reay had no other commitments at the time and Padua seemed as good a place to be in as anywhere else, so he accepted the devil's invitation, sallied off to Italy, and became enrolled as a student in devilish matters at Padua.

Everything went well for a while. His lordship acquired a trick or two of devilment and enjoyed very much the carousing in the taverns of Padua that provided the students with their relaxation.

One day, however, the devil announced that the end of term was in sight and that this would be celebrated in the traditional manner of educational establishments with the presentation of prizes for intellectual and sporting achievements. One of the events of the day would be a race round the school buildings, in which the last to enter the school hall would go to the devil.

Owing to his style of life, Lord Reay did not shine in athletic pursuits, and as the students streamed through the corridors of the educational establishment, he realized that he was coming a good last. Panting and gasping as he ran upstairs and downstairs and in and out of the classrooms, Lord Reay racked his brains to find a way of evading the devil's clutches and just as he staggered last through the hall doors, the idea came to him.

'The devil take the hindmost!' he roared as, summoning up a last burst of speed, he sped past the devil's waiting arms. The satanic headship, thinking that there was someone behind Lord Reay, almost missed his victim, but not quite. Realizing that he had been duped, he made a desperate grab at the fleeing figure of his lordship but only managed to catch the tail end of his shadow which separated itself from its owner with a sound like the rending of linen.

This narrow escape upset Lord Reay to such an extent that he now longed for a quiet life at his home in the north of Scotland. He did not at all regret leaving the warm climes of Italy for the damp mistiness of his native land. Indeed, the lack of sunshine was something to be welcomed because, having left his shadow in the devil's hands, he now possessed the peculiarity of being shadowless – a characteristic that was bound to attract attention and arouse gossip.

Having settled himself down in the Mackay lands near the Smoo Cave, Lord Reay looked forward to growing old gracefully and in tranquillity. The devil had other ideas. Wrapping Lord Reay's shadow in a bag with clothes for the journey, the devil travelled to Smoo where he waylaid Lord Reay one day as he was walking along the cliffs. Angry words quickly turned to blows, and soon the devil and Lord Reay were wrestling perilously on the edge of the cliff. Indignation at being molested on his own lands by a foreign intruder lent Lord Reay strength. Soon he had the devil at his mercy, only releasing him on the promise that not only would the devil cease to bother him but that he would also supply him with a staff of hard-working demons to help him maintain his house and look after his farm.

Nursing his damaged pride, the devil retired to the Smoo Cave where he received hospitality from a band of friendly witches who had little love for Lord Reay. Together, they planned to ambush the Lord in the caves. Sending him a message that he would hear something to his interest if he visited the caves, the band of conspirators waited.

It was not long before one of their outposts sent word that Lord Reay had left his home and was on his way. This message did not add that Lord Reay was accompanied by his faithful dog who possessed that sixth sense of all good hunting dogs. As soon as they were in the caves, the dog, sensing that something was not right, went ahead of his master into the inner cave, where the devil and the witches waited. The shock the poor creature received made him instantly lose all his hair.

When Lord Reay saw his dog return as a whimpering and hairless monstrosity, he knew that only one person could be responsible and his anger overflowed. Striding forward with footsteps that shook the walls of the cavern and shouting imprecations that even the devil had not heard before Lord Reay threatened that if he caught hold of the devil he would not only tear him limb from limb but would boil him in oil and turn his skin into a hearth rug.

On hearing this, the devil withdrew deeper and deeper into the cave until there was nowhere else for him to go. Lord Reay's footsteps came nearer and nearer. There seemed no escape for old Nicodemus, but calling on all his devilish power, he blew a hole through the roof of the cave and shot off through the midnight sky as fast as he could go.

And this is why the Smoo Cave has a hole in its roof and why the devil is not seen around these parts any more.

THE WALK:
FROM DURNESS, VIA BALNAKIEL VILLAGE TO FARAID HEAD.

MAP SQUARE:
Ordnance Survey Sheet 9/404678
Much of this 6½ mile walk is along a beach and over sand dunes.

Durness and Balnakiel are about as far north as civilization reaches in mainland Scotland; in fact, Durness is Britain's most northerly mainland parish. Cape Wrath is a lonely and hilly drive away on a minor road from the ferry across the Kyle of Durness. Durness lies on the A838 which circles north-western Scotland from Lairg.

We are assuming that you will have stopped at Smoo, where there is a hotel, to visit the Cave, so we are suggesting for the Lord Reay country a walk from Durness, a mile and a half west of Smoo on the A838.

The walk begins by the Information office in Durness, which is at the junction of the A838 and the Balnakiel road. Take the Balnakiel road through the village for just under a mile, when you will come to a T-junction.

On the left is the Balnakiel Craft Village, sited in an old RAF station. It is open daily from Easter to the end of September and is well worth a visit. Crafts being demonstrated usually include pottery, weaving, metalwork and even boatbuilding. There are also a coffee shop and hotel here.

The right-hand turning at the T-junction passes the coastguard lookout and, after a quarter of a mile, reaches Balnakiel, a name which means 'Place of the Kirk'.

The village sits neatly in the south-east corner of Balnakiel Bay and is fringed by a curved beach and shallow seas. On your right as you walk through the village you will see the crow-stepped gabled Balnakiel House, sitting by a small stream. This once belonged to the Lords Reay.

On the left of the road, the ruined and roofless church of Durness, built in 1619, stands in its stone-walled graveyard. Among the gravestones is that of Rob Dunn Calder, or Robb Donn, the Gaelic poet who was buried here in 1777. In the church is a monument to one Donald Makmurchov, carved with a skull and crossbones and an archer killing a deer.

Once through the village, keep to the eastern shore of Balnakiel Bay. Due north ahead of you lie nearly two miles of beach and vast sand dunes, with a track at the northern end of the beach to take you over dunes covered with marram grass to

Faraid Head. From the windswept 330-feet headland, if the day is clear, you will have fine views across the Kyle of Durness to Cape Wrath, along the coast to Eriboll in the east, and inland to the Reay forest.

The return route to Durness retraces your outward journey, though at Balnakiel there is another track that cuts east across the bottom of Faraid Head to the cliff tops at Aodann Mhor and then south to Durness. Taking this track back to Durness would add about three-quarters of a mile to the walk.

6. THE DEVIL AND MACLEOD OF ASSYNT
Ardvreck Castle, Loch Assynt

Loch Assynt lies to the west of the A894 north of Ullapool in one of the most beautiful corners of the Highlands. To its north lies the mountain called Quinag (2653 feet) and to the south is Beinn Gharbhand and Canisp (2779 feet) and Suilven (2399 feet). The A837 which branches off the main road and runs east along the north side of Loch Assynt is the beginning of two spectacular drives. The starting point of each of them is at Lochinver, eleven miles away and a popular centre for holidays in Assynt, whose harbour is a meeting place for fishing boats from all along the coast.

To the north, the road circles parallel to the coast and rejoins the A894 near the Kylesku ferry; to the south, the circuit encloses the superb landscapes of the Glencanisp and the Inverpolly forests. This is all wonderful country for walks or scrambling up the mountains whose sides appear to rise sheer from the wooded lochans but which all have relatively easy paths to their summits.

Loch Assynt itself has much of the individuality of character of the mountains. At its western end it is a wooded loch, curving gently towards the River Inver which reaches the sea at Lochinver; to the east, the loch shore is stark and treeless, providing a fitting backdrop for the crumbling silhouette of the once great Ardvreck Castle, built in 1597 and seat of the MacLeods of Assynt, a sept of the MacLeods of Lewis and therefore related to the MacLeods of Skye.

Envy of the Dunvegan MacLeods was the downfall of the MacLeods of Assynt; according to legend, it happened like this.

Eaten by envy of the beautiful castle of the MacLeods of

43

Ardvreck Castle at the East of Loch Assynt.

Dunvegan on Skye (see the Faery Flag, page 81), MacLeod of Assynt made up his mind that he would equal the rival branch of his family in power and splendour. Unable to achieve his ambition by his own efforts, MacLeod called upon the devil's help. Always ready to oblige, the devil agreed to discuss the matter, and accepted MacLeod's invitation to a dinner at which they would talk. MacLeod explained to the devil that his desires were simply to have a larger castle than the MacLeods of Skye and, of course, to have the means to maintain it in an appropriate style.

The devil, having supped well, waved the glass of brandy with which his host had provided him, and assured him that there was no problem at all in bringing about MacLeod's wishes. There was just one little thing; the agreement that would seal their deal would necessarily contain a small clause under which the devil, in return for his help, would become the owner of MacLeod's soul on his death.

'After all,' the devil said agreeably, 'you, yourself, will have no more use for it.'

Though he was quite prepared to make a deal with the devil to score off the MacLeods of Dunvegan, the chief of the MacLeods of Assynt felt this was going too far. He was also a cunning negotiator, however, and did not reject the devil's 'small clause' out of hand.

'Very well,' he said. 'But there is just one other small clause that I should like to add. That is that one of the gifts that you will grant me is the gift of immortality.'

'I see,' said the devil. 'Well, let us talk about it.'

And so they did, long into the night and into the next day when they were suddenly aware that all the castle was coming to life and that there was nothing they desired more than a long, hot drink and some fresh-baked bread.

MacLeod clapped his hands and shouted for someone to bring food and drink. After a while the door opened and there, with a tray of bread and jug of steaming hot milk, was the prettiest, purest girl that the devil had ever seen. He fell in love with her at first sight.

'My daughter,' said MacLeod. When the girl had left the room he asked the devil why he suddenly seemed so distracted.

'I was thinking,' the devil said, 'that I will agree to everything you say and put only one condition of my own.'

'And what is that?' MacLeod asked.

'That I may marry your daughter.'

MacLeod was taken aback but the prospect of having his wishes granted at no risk at all to himself made him agree at once before the devil could change his mind.

And that is how the devil came to marry MacLeod's daughter and how the MacLeods of Assynt became owners of the large and splendid Ardvreck Castle on Loch Assynt.

When MacLeod's daughter discovered that her husband was the devil himself she was appalled at what her father had done and she began to pine. Nothing that the devil could do could restore her once-cheerful spirits and her health declined until she was a mere shadow of her former self. Finally, she died and since her soul had not been promised to the devil she became free.

The enormity of her father's betrayal was something that she could never understand, and even though she was now dead and free of the devil, she continued to wander about Ardvreck Castle trying to explain to herself how a father could do such a terrible thing to his daughter. People say that her pale and sad shade may be seen haunting the ruins to this day.

The devil, too, seems to have continued to hover over the MacLeods of Assynt. It was at Ardvreck Castle that Neil MacLeod, the eleventh chief of the line, desperately in debt, held the great Montrose prisoner in 1650 and delivered him to the Covenanters for £20,000.

Montrose was hanged at Edinburgh but MacLeod gained nothing for his crime. Cromwell's government never paid him, except to give him 400 bolls of sour meal, and his act aroused the Mackenzie clan to take revenge for

The Ruins of Ardvreck Castle.

46

the treatment of the Scottish hero and supporter of Charles II. They descended on Assynt, causing great devastation before seizing it for themselves. MacLeod was imprisoned and though later released never regained the castle for which his ancestor had paid so high a price.

THE WALK:
FROM INCHNADAMPH
VIA THE RIVER
TRALIGILL TO LOCH
MHAOLACH-COIRE IN
THE INCHNADAMPH
NATIONAL NATURE
RESERVE, AND BACK TO
INCHNADAMPH ON THE
SAME PATH.

MAP SQUARE:
Ordnance Survey Sheet
15/251218
A 4½ mile walk at the western foot of Ben More Assynt, Sutherland's highest mountain.

There is no railway in this part of Scotland, but bus services do reach Loch Assynt and Lochinver. To explore the beautiful landscape around Loch Assynt and to the south, where the great Torridon sandstone peaks rise to the sky, you will probably make your base in Lochinver or Ullapool, where there are several good hotels; and there is also a hotel in Inchnadamph at the eastern end of the loch which is popular with walkers, geologists and fishermen.

A glance at the Ordnance Survey map of the Loch Assynt region will reveal many paths among the hills and mountains at the eastern end of the loch, for this is geologically very interesting country.

The 3200-acre Inchnadamph National Nature Reserve, which lies just south of the village, contains within its border limestone caves in which have been found vestiges of human habitation dating back to 6000 BC – the earliest traces so far discovered of human settlement in Scotland. These caves lie just south of the Allt nan Uamh about a mile upstream from where the A837 crosses it two and a half miles south of

Inchnadamph. There is no marked path to the caves, but they are not difficult to reach.

Limestone caves also feature on the walk we have chosen to describe here. This one does have a clear path to follow and is, perhaps, more interesting for walkers without specialized geological or speleological knowledge as the ground is varied and there are several sites of interest en route. This walk begins in Inchnadamph village and follows the course of the Traligill river before heading south to Loch Mhaolach-coire in the Nature Reserve.

The starting point is the beginning of the track that leads east (that is away from the loch shore) off the A837 just north of the bridge over the Traligill. (The Inchnadamph Hotel, which has a petrol pump in its car park, is just the other side of the bridge.)

At first just a gentle uphill slope as it passes village buildings, the track soon begins a more obvious climb uphill. Half a mile from the start, the track crosses a burn, the Allt Poll an Droighinn, which flows into the Traligill. Just beyond, a cairn stands between the track and the river, and shortly past this the track becomes a path. At the point – about one and a half miles from the start of the walk – where the Traligill suddenly disappears underground, to re-emerge a few hundred yards downstream, the path turns south away from the river and Gleann Dubh. Walk on for a quarter of a mile, and you will reach three limestone caves. There are stalactites in one of the caves, which you can get into, though its ceiling is too low to allow you to stand upright in many parts. Never touch the stalactites – in fact, treat them as if they were the rarest and most delicate porcelain: they took many thousands of years to form and cannot be replaced if you break them.

The final section of the outward journey of this walk is the quarter-mile stretch of path to Loch Mhaolach-coire, across the lower slopes of Ben More Assynt and its attendant peaks, crossing a small burn on the way.

THE NORTH-WESTERN HIGHLANDS

7. McCRAE AND THE WITCHES
Ardelve

One of the Roads to the Isles, the A87 from Invergarry in the Great Glen to Kyle of Lochalsh, the embarkation point for Skye, runs along the north side of Loch Alsh, passing by the village of Ardelve. All around the village there are superb views of wooded hills and mountains, and of stretches of Loch Alsh and Loch Duich.

Kyle of Lochalsh.

At one time the whole of Loch Alsh was a wonderful fishing ground and fishermen and their families formed the largest proportion of the population of the villages built along the shore. Ardelve was one such village. There, according to legend, there once lived a fisherman called McCrae.

Like most fishermen, McCrae looked after his boat very carefully, keeping it well maintained because it was his means of livelihood. Whenever any of its timbers needed replacing he would go off to the surrounding forests to cut himself a suitable piece of wood which he would then season until it was ready.

One day, while on one of these expeditions, McCrae was overtaken so quickly by one of those Scottish mists that blot out the landscape that he lost his way. As he stumbled about among the trees hoping he was going in the right direction, McCrae saw a light. By this time, he was exhausted as well as hungry and thirsty, so decided to knock at the door of the house and ask for hospitality and permission to stop the night there.

McCrae knocked on the door, quietly at first and then louder until finally he banged his strong fist against the timbers until the house shook. At long last, the door opened and an old woman asked him what he wanted. 'Just a bit of food and shelter, if it is not asking too much,' McCrae said. He did not much like the look of the old woman and had it not been such a bad night he would have walked on. The old woman was now beckoning him into the house, so he thought he might as well enter.

He found himself in a low-ceilinged, smoke-filled room lit by candles. On a large table in the centre sat a huge black cat and on the chairs beyond it with their backs to him were two other old women staring at the smoking fire which filled the hearth. The old woman who had invited him in motioned to him to sit down and pushed some bread and cheese towards him and then joined her companions at the fireplace. After an attempt or two to make conversation, McCrae subsided into silence. When he had eaten he folded his arms on the table and, putting his head on them, fell asleep.

He was awakened by the sound of the old women whispering, and being a cautious man in some respects, he did not immediately sit up and reveal that he was awake. Instead, he opened one eye and peered cautiously at the three old crones. What he saw surprised him. The women sat around a wooden box by the fire and one of them extracted from it a blue knitted cap which she placed on her head. As she did so she muttered the word 'Carlisle' three times and on the third, to McCrae's utter amazement, she vanished. McCrae moved never a muscle but his eye remained glued on the other women, one of whom now repeated her companion's trick. It was evident to McCrae that he had fallen in with witches and he remained quieter than ever until the third one had disappeared.

Then and only then did McCrae stand up and, moving carefully round the table, peered into the wooden box. There, at the bottom of it, lay another blue cap.

McCrae stared at it for a time and then a daring and amusing thought came into his head. Suppose he stole this cap? What a trick it would play on his friends when he got back to Ardelve! He picked the cap up gingerly and, seeing that no harm came to him, he put it on his head. Again nothing happened.

'Carlisle,' said McCrae. 'Carlisle.' And for the third time, 'Carlisle.'

Without knowing quite how it had happened McCrae now found himself on the stone floor of a room without windows. At first he thought he had fallen into a dungeon. Then, as his eyes became accustomed to the dark, he saw that the walls of the room were lined with bottles and that there were racks of bottles right across the floor. He was in a wine cellar.

Recovering from his amazement, McCrae began to examine the bottles, which were of the finest claret and burgundy. The more he looked, the thirstier he became and since there was no one to prevent him he opened one of the bottles and drank its contents.

53

Next morning, when the keepers of the cellar of the Bishop of Carlisle, for that is whom it belonged to, arrived to take out the Bishop's daily requirements they found McCrae asleep and snoring, with an assortment of empty bottles scattered round him. The men gave a cry of dismay which summoned the guard who immediately arrested McCrae and took him up to the castle courtyard where he was summarily tried and sentenced to death.

McCrae's explanation of how he happened to be in the Bishop's cellar only made matters worse, for his captors now not only believed that he had designs on the Bishop's life but also thought that he was some kind of witch as well, and he was condemned to death by burning.

As he stood tied to the stake and the Bishop's servants piled up timber around him, McCrae wished that he had never put on the witches' blue cap. Blue cap. Suddenly McCrae thought of his only possible means of escape.

Begging that a last wish might be granted, to which his captors agreed, he asked that the blue cap that was in his pocket might be put on his head. Shrugging at such a trivial request, the men placed the cap on McCrae's head whereupon he immediately and rapidly cried out 'Kintail, Kintail, Kintail!' At the third naming of the region in which Ardelve lies, McCrae found himself among the trees of a wood alongside Loch Alsh.

There was only one impediment to his running home; he was still tied to the stake at which he had narrowly escaped burning. It was not long before a woodman came by and, seeing McCrae lying on the ground roped to a stake, asked him what he was about.

'It's like this,' McCrae said, 'I was taking this timber home to mend my boat and I fell.'

There is no record of what his good samaritan thought of this explanation but McCrae got home with his blue cap. He never ever called out 'Carlisle' again.

THE WALKS:	MAP SQUARE:

THE WALKS:
1. FROM ARDELVE TO ALLT-NAN-SUGH ON LOCH LONG.
2. A WALK IN THE NATIONAL TRUST FOR SCOTLAND'S LOCHALSH WOODLAND GARDENS.

MAP SQUARE:
1. Ordnance Survey Sheet 33/878267
2. Ordnance Survey Sheet 33/802278

Two short and not difficult walks which give fine introductions to the beautiful scenery around Ardelve.

Ardelve lies 7½ miles east of Kyle of Lochalsh. By car it can be reached on the A87(T) either from Kyle of Lochalsh or from the direction of the Great Glen.

Ardelve is a small collection of cottages on the west side of the bridge which carries the main road over the meeting point of Lochs Alsh, Duich and Long at Dornie.

The FIRST SUGGESTED WALK in the area is just over five and a half miles and begins at Ardelve. You can leave your car at the car park on Ardelve Point. Follow the A87(T) a few yards north to the right-hand turning almost directly opposite the Loch Duich Hotel and camping site. This skirts the buildings of Camas-Longart on the edge of Loch Long for about three-quarters of a mile until it meets the minor road to Killilan which follows the western shore of Loch Long. Turn right on to this road and walk to Allt-nan-sugh, just under two miles away. The walk, which gives good views of the quiet beauty of Loch Long, is also under the shadow of the steep slopes of Beinn Conchra (1510 feet), down whose sides several streams flow into the loch.

We suggest you turn back to Ardelve at this point, though you could walk the length of Loch Long to Killilan, about three miles away. (A really long and strenuous walk would take you all the way to the Falls of Glomach via Killilan House, the Allt a' Glomaich and the steep ascent to the Falls themselves.)

The SECOND SUGGESTED WALK here is in the Woodland Garden established by the National Trust for

Scotland in six-and-a-half acres of Lochalsh House's grounds, which lie along the edge of Loch Alsh off the A87(T) just west of Balmacara Square. The entrance is well signposted and a NTS flag flies at the gate of the gardens, which are open all year.

Footpaths have been laid out in the woodland, which is a mixture of mature Scots pine, larch, oak and beech, and newer plantings of pine and spruce, handsome rhododendrons, and exotics from Australia, New Zealand, Chile, the Himalayas and the Far East.

Two viewpoints offer fine views across Loch Alsh and a Visitor Centre includes displays which help the visitor identify things seen on the walks.

The Woodland Garden is very lovely and well worth a visit.

Having mentioned the National Trust for Scotland here, we should tell you about the Trust's Balmacara Estate which consists of 5616 acres of land on the Kyle–Plockton peninsula. Here, the Trust offers several walks guided by rangers/naturalists who tell walkers about the social and natural history of the region as well as guiding them on walks with superb hill and coastal scenery. The Trust's Balmacara Information Centre is on the A87(T) three-quarters of a mile west of Kirton.

8. THE SEAL PRINCESSES
Loch Duich

The famous castle of Eilean Donan, once a stronghold of the Mackenzies of Kintail, stands on an island (now joined to the mainland) at the junction of Loch Alsh, Loch Long and Loch Duich. It is one of the most splendidly situated of all Scottish castles and from the slopes and peaks of the mountains that crowd in on the lochs there are superb views down Loch Alsh to the Isle of Skye and the open sea and eastwards to the upper reaches of Loch Duich where the range known as the Five Sisters of Kintail rises majestically above pinewoods.

The castle has all the appearance of an ancient Highland stronghold, so it is all the more surprising to learn that it was reconstructed as recently as the 1930s after having lain in ruins since 1719. It was destroyed by a Royal Navy man-of-war after the abortive Jacobite uprising of 1719 in which its masters, the Mackenzies, and their Spanish allies had been involved. Nevertheless, it has an air of authenticity which helps conjure up a vivid image of those turbulent times when the Scottish clans were always at odds with each other or with the central government and their sovereign.

At the junction of the three lochs lies the village of Dornie alongside the bridge across Loch Long which carries the A87(T) from Kyle of Lochalsh to Fort William. Dornie was once an important fishing village and the fishermen's cottages were strung out along the shores of Loch Duich for several miles. The men living in the sheltered waters of the loch sailed out along Loch Alsh to the seas around the Isle of Skye where the abundant shoals of fish provided them with a living. As with most seagoing

Loch Duich.

people, they were good at spinning a yarn. One of these, passed on from generation to generation, was the story of the three seal princesses of the loch.

In one of the cottages along the loch there lived three brothers whose ageing mother looked after all their needs, cooking, sewing and keeping the cottage clean for them. In fact, she did this so well that none of the brothers had any desire to leave home and start a place of his own. Their mother had other ideas, however. She longed for each of them to get some other woman to take over the chores and constantly encouraged them to find themselves wives. The years went by and the brothers began to build other cottages of their own to house their wives, but that was as far as they went for they evidently enjoyed their bachelor lives and were in no hurry to end them.

One evening, as they returned up the loch from Kyle of Lochalsh where they had been enjoying the company of some of the local girls and, no doubt, drinking a dram or two, they saw an amazing sight on one of the beaches near their home. The shore was alive with seals that were leaving the water and, discarding their sealskins, transforming themselves into the most attractive young men and women that the brothers had ever seen. Unable to believe their eyes, the brothers quietly beached their boat and sat down to watch from behind some nearby boulders.

It was evident from their behaviour that the seal people were expecting someone important to make an appearance for as they chatted and laughed they kept gazing down the loch towards the sea. Suddenly, three figures appeared swimming slowly towards the beach and all the seal people crowded round to help the newcomers ashore. In their midst, the brothers now saw three beautiful golden-haired girls who walked through the avenue which opened up in the crowd and gave a signal for dancing and feasting to begin.

These, as the brothers soon guessed, were the seal princesses and they were instantly bewitched by them to such an extent that, though the possibility seemed a remote one, they determined to get to know them better. But how did human beings get close to seal princesses? The problem filled the brothers' minds for some weeks, during which they spent many hours watching the seal people. Then the eldest of the brothers had a brainwave. On coming ashore, the seal people always discarded their seal skins; therefore, it seemed reasonable to suppose that without their skins they could not return to the sea.

The next time the brothers saw the seals, they had a plan of action already worked out.

As soon as the seal princesses discarded their skins, the brothers carefully noted the place where they had laid them among the other skins, and, while the seal people were enjoying their dancing, they crept out of their hiding place and stole the princesses' skins.

When the night's festivities drew to a close, the seals all

donned their skins and slid back into the water and down Loch Alsh – all that is, but the princesses. After searching high and low for their skins, they sat disconsolately on a rock by the water's edge in despair. How would they ever get home without their skins and what would their parents say? As they talked to each other in low, unhappy voices the brothers walked slowly towards them calling to them not to be afraid for they were there to help them.

The three brothers each led one of the captive princesses to his own house, but the youngest brother found himself unable to go through with the plan he and his brothers had hatched. Though reluctant to let his beautiful prisoner go, he told her where he had hidden her seal skin and when he woke in the morning she had gone. When his brothers heard what he had done they jeered at him for his feeblemindedness and made even more sure that the skins of their own princesses were hidden where they could never be found.

Nine days after the disappearance of his princess, the youngest brother woke to the sound of a tap on his door and, opening it, found to his surprise that it was his seal princess. She spent the night in his cottage but in the morning she had gone. This happened every ninth night and the younger brother came to accept that this was the only way in which he could share the princess's life. On these nights, the other brothers locked and barricaded the doors and windows of their cottages in case the seal people found a way of liberating their captives.

In the course of time, the seal princesses all gave birth to children. The two elder brothers' domestic problems increased for not only did they have unhappy wives, but they also had children who spent all their time swimming in the loch showing no interest in their fathers' work.

One day, the children's curiosity led them to the secret place where their fathers had hidden the seal skins. Digging them out, they took them back to their mothers.

That night, when the brothers returned from their fishing, they found their wives and their children had gone. They never saw them again. The younger brother, however, continued to see his seal wife every ninth night and their children shared their lives equally with both parents.

This is the Loch Duich legend but many other stories about seal princesses may be heard all around the shores of Scotland, where seals abound even to this day. They may be seen in the waters and on the rocks off Kintyre, the isle of Islay, the islands of Mull and Skye, on the coasts of the outer Hebrides and along the shores of Sutherland. Some of them may even dance on the shore by the light of the moon. Who knows?

THE WALK:	MAP SQUARE:
FROM DORNIE, PAST EILEAN DONAN CASTLE TO CARR BRAE AND KEPPOCH, THEN ON TO INVERINATE, OR BACK TO DORNIE.	Ordnance Survey Sheet 33/879263 This walk is suggested for its glorious views of loch, sea and mountains.

Loch Duich and Dornie lie on the A87(T) to Kyle of Lochalsh, and are served by two bus services from Edinburgh to Skye. The nearest railway station is Kyle of Lochalsh.

The country round Loch Duich can offer some excellent walking. The walk suggested here begins at the old fishing village of Dornie. You can leave your car in the car park at Ardelve Point and walk over the bridge to Dornie. After visiting Eilean Donan, which is open daily from Easter to September, take the minor road, sign-posted 'Carrbrae View Point', that goes uphill from where the A87(T) bends south east along the loch.

This minor road which runs parallel to the A87(T) takes you high enough up the side of the surrounding hills to provide splendid views over the loch and hills. Immediately below you, Eilean Donan stands just offshore on its small island, linked to the shore by a causeway. Farther away beyond Loch Alsh lies Skye, and on a fine day the peaks of the Cuillins stand out clearly. South-east, beyond the head of Loch Duich, the Five Sisters range and the mountains and ridges of the Glenshiel Forest close the view.

Leaving the viewpoint above Eilean Donan, you can carry on along the road, which is fairly steep and tree-lined at first and then reaches more open, hilly and grass-covered country, to Carr Brae, a mile-and-a-quarter farther on. Here there is another fine viewpoint, and then on for another mile-and-a-half to the junction where our minor road rejoins the A87(T).

9. THE SEVEN SISTERS OF KINTAIL
Loch Duich

In the great stony landscape that abuts on the Inner Sound of Skye the mountains crowd together around the lochs, their rounded heads dropping steeply towards the water's edge. Here and there thick forests clothe the lower slopes and along the lochs wildlife lives in profusion. Seals may be seen on the rocks, herons fly lazily from one vantage point to another, and other sea birds are commonly seen. At the point nearest to the Isle of Skye is Kyle of Lochalsh, the terminal for car and passenger ferries to the island, lying at the western end of the loch of the same name. As you follow Loch Alsh inland to Dornie, you cross a bridge on the other side of which is the old stone-cottage fishing village of Dornie, hugging the shore of Loch Long at the point where it joins Loch Duich. The splendidly restored castle of Eilean Donan stands offshore just east of Dornie at the point where the three fiord lochs, Alsh, Long and Duich, converge.

From here eastwards the scenery becomes more and more breathtaking until it reaches Glen Shiel. On the south banks of the loch Ratagan Forest throws a dark green patch across the hillside, and through it runs the road to Glenelg over a 1116-feet pass giving superb views over Loch Duich. At the head of the loch is the Morvich camping site where an audio/visual exhibition has been set up to tell visitors about the loch and its surrounding countryside.

Beyond lie Beinn Fada (3383 feet) and its five great spurs, the Five Sisters of Kintail. The mountains, now owned by the National Trust, were once part of the MacKenzie lands, and perhaps it was during the time of their MacKenzie ownership that the events took place

The Five Sisters of Kintail.

which gave the Five Sisters their name.

According to the story, a man of Kintail who lived on Loch Duich had seven beautiful daughters. The girls were not only beautiful but also considerate to their father whom they looked after, doing his cooking, mending his clothes and helping him with his fishing gear. Until they were in their teens, they were happy enough and found living at home sufficient to fill their lives, but then they began to dream of handsome young men and to wish they could meet some.

This was not an easy matter, for Loch Duich did not have a large population and the few boys they did meet failed to live up to their expectations. Then, one day a ship sailed into the loch. It had evidently been through a storm, for its mast had snapped and the lines and rigging hung from the yardarms in a tangle. The sisters watched the ship drop anchor and saw a boat lowered. As it approached the shore, they were able to make out that two handsome, golden-haired youths were rowing it in their direction. The sisters were very excited at the appearance of the two strangers and, as soon as the two young men had leapt ashore, invited them up to their house to meet their father.

They learnt that the ship was indeed badly damaged and that the youths needed help to repair it before they could set off again for their home in Ireland. During the days that followed, the seven sisters and the two boys came to know each other well but, though they all played and worked together in harmony, it soon became evident that the boys had eyes only for the two youngest girls.

Time passed and the ship was ready to sail again but no one looked on the departure with great joy, not even the boys, although they wanted to get home, for they had fallen in love with the two youngest sisters and were reluctant to leave them. The boys conferred with each other, then approached the father and asked if they could take the young sisters with them as their brides.

The father had no objection, for he had come to like the lads, but he found that he now had to face a storm of protest from the other sisters, who envied the youngest ones' good fortune. The two sisters were naturally upset at their oldest sisters' attitude and, because they had always been a close family, were almost prepared to give up their plan to sail away with the brothers rather than create a rift with their sisters which would also upset their father.

When the brothers heard about the family discussions the elder of them spoke up. He explained that they had five older brothers back home in Ireland, all of whom looked very much like themselves and that in return for having the family blessing on their union with the younger sisters they would arrange for their brothers to sail over the sea to meet the five sisters who were left. At this offer, the five sisters withdrew their objections to the match between their younger sisters and the brothers and after a wedding feast they all went down to the shore and saw the two happy young couples off to Ireland.

Weeks went by, then months, but there was no sign of the five brothers. The five sisters became extremely unhappy, so much so that their father began to worry about them. Not knowing what to do, he consulted a local wizard. The wizard looked into a lochan that served as his crystal ball and meditated for a whole night before he visited the five sisters and told them that he had seen no sign of the five brothers and that as far as he could make out the two who had visited Loch Duich had no other brothers or sisters.

His words fell on deaf ears, for the sisters were convinced that the brothers would arrive one day and nobody could persuade them that the two fair youths whom they had last seen sailing away with their youngest sisters were liars. Their father tried for weeks to persuade them to give up their hopeless wait but they were adamant. One day their blond lovers would come.

Their father was reluctant to tell them that they would become old and ugly with waiting so he went to the wizard again for advice. Once more the wizard pondered long on what to do. Next day, he called on the five sisters and told them it was possible the brothers would take years to arrive and that when they eventually appeared they would be expecting to find five beautiful girls waiting for them but instead would find five old hags. He then hastened to explain to them that he had a plan which would enable them to remain beautiful forever. The father, to whom the wizard had already confided his plan, looked anxious, for he did not entirely like the idea, but if it made his daughters happy that was enough for him.

The wizard explained his plan at length and the sisters listened. They were prepared to wait forever for their lovers but they wanted to be beautiful for them when they arrived. They looked at each other and agreed. The wizard began his spellmaking and gradually the transformation that he had promised them took place. When it was finished, there at the end of Loch Duich stood five beautiful mountains that, since that time generations ago when the spell was cast, have had not five but millions of lovers who have been bewitched by their beauty.

THE WALKS:	MAP SQUARE:
1. FROM MORVICH ALONG THE BANKS OF THE RIVER CROE.	1. Ordnance Survey Sheet 33/962211
2. FROM MORVICH UP STRATH CROE TO THE FALLS OF GLOMACH.	2. Ordnance Survey Sheet 33/962211 The first walk can be as long as you like. The second is a harder 7-mile walk.

The A87(T) from Fort William passes to the west of the Five Sisters of Kintail and continues north along Loch Duich and west along Loch Alsh to Kyle of Lochalsh. The railway reaches Kyle of Lochalsh via Loch Carron, so there is no line via the Five Sisters, but there are bus services to the area.

About 13,000 acres of countryside round the Five Sisters are protected by the National Trust for Scotland, including Beinn Fhada and the Falls of Glomach. This is very fine walking country, with a wild grandeur, where herds of red deer and goats roam wild, and where the views of mountain and loch are superb.

Morvich, on Loch Duich, where there are camp and caravan sites, and an information centre, is a good starting point for walks in the area.

The FIRST SUGGESTED WALK can be as long as you want to make it, for it follows the banks of the River Croe up Gleann Lichd. The whole distance from Morvich to the head of the glen is about five miles. Steep and rugged mountains rise on either side of the glen, the Five Sisters of Kintail to the south-west and the great mass of the Beinn Fhada (or Ben Attow, as it is also known) range to the north-east. Many small streams drain down into the river. The minor road and track up the glen follows the south-western bank of the river. If you walk to the head of the glen you will find a country of breath-taking grandeur and ruggedness. Up here is the watershed between Scotland's eastern and western seas, and the drop into Gleann Lichd is very steep and marked by an impressive waterfall.

A waterfall, the Falls of Glomach, is also the target of the SECOND SUGGESTED WALK in the area of the Five Sisters. The Falls of Glomach are the second highest in Britain, and drop 370 feet in one plunge. They can be a disappointment, however, especially if there has been little rain. As this walk is at least a two-hour hard slog over seven miles of forest and moorland from Morvich to the Falls, it is not something to be undertaken lightly. On the other hand, the walker's path to it is clear and easy to follow, and the country is spectacular. The walk proper begins at Croe Bridge, near the Morvich information centre and camping site, as this is the nearest convenient car parking area to the start of the walk proper.

From Croe Bridge, walk north along the road to a minor metalled road in poor condition going off to the right to Ruarach Farm. This road brings you to a wall and a gate from which you will get your first good views of the green valley ahead. Beyond the gate, you pass a cluster of farm buildings sitting among trees. Ahead, the great mountains of Kintail tower over the broad, steep-sided valley, Strath Croe.

At Dorusduain, nearly two miles from Ruarach Farm, the path to the Falls of Glomach turns left through the wood, climbing steeply up a ravine, and emerges into a steep, treeless valley which leads over the pass, Bealach na Sroine, to the Falls of Glomach.

If you do not want to take the hard slog to the Falls of Glomach but want to carry on walking, you have the choice of something easier at Dorusduain. You can cross the river here and follow the path east up Gleann Choinneachain to another, though less spectacular, waterfall. This path is about a mile-and-three-quarters in length.

10. THE GIANTS OF LOCH SHIEL
Loch Shiel

The Lochaber district of the Highlands covers the south-west corner of Inverness-shire and stretches to the Atlantic coast. Its steep mountains and narrow glens are the evocative setting for many legendary tales. Some, like those surrounding Prince Charles Stuart, have a basis in historical fact, but many others are the product of the imaginative Celtic mind.

To the south-east of Lochaber rises the awesome mass of Ben Nevis, the highest mountain in Britain, and in the west, running parallel to the Great Glen which cuts diagonally across northern Scotland, is Loch Shiel, an eighteen-mile-long freshwater loch that is no more than a mile wide at its broadest point. At the head of the loch is Glen Finnan where Charles raised his standard and rallied the clans to his cause in 1745.

At this point, the Road to the Isles cuts across the head of the loch through a steep-sided glen. The sides of the loch are equally steep, rising to rocky summits like Beinn Odhar Mor (870 feet) on the western side and Sgorr Craobh a Chaorainn (722 feet) on the east. Their ridges are covered in outcrops of weathered rocks, and it was these scatterings of rock which gave rise to the legend of the giants of Loch Shiel.

In ancient times, according to the legend, the quarrelsome giants inhabited the hills surrounding the loch, along whose shores most of the best agricultural land was strewn with boulders. These prevented the human inhabitants of the country from cultivating the land, so the people were poor as well as terrorized by the thumps and crashes of the aggressive giants whose daily encounters echoed around the glen as they tried to outdo each other in wrestling and feats of strength.

One day, however, a local sage who had spent his life in meditation had a brilliant idea. If, he reasoned, the giants were so determined to prove to each other who was the stronger of the two, why not put their energy and aggressiveness to good use. He then set about persuading the giants that a real test of their power would be to see how many boulders they could throw out of the most fertile glen along the loch shore on to the mountain tops.

If they would come down from their mountains to where all the local people could see them, the sage pointed out, all the world would know which giant was the stronger.

Ready for any opportunity to prove their superiority, the giants set about clearing the glen. For a whole day they contested for the name of the strongest. Up and down the glen they strode, hurling ever larger boulders up into the air and over the mountain tops. By nightfall the giants had cleared the glen, but . . . who was the stronger?

The sage decided that the only way to settle this point was to find which rock had fallen the furthest away from the glen. The two giants, maybe too exhausted to think properly or maybe just not very bright, set off over the mountains to find the most distant rock. No one living around Loch Shiel has seen them from that day to this.

THE WALK:	MAP SQUARE:
FROM GLENFINNAN	Ordnance Survey Sheet
VILLAGE NORTH UP	40/907807
GLEN FINNAN, AND BACK	A 7-mile walk in the footsteps
TO THE VILLAGE.	of Bonnie Prince Charlie.

St Finan, a sixth-century monk of great piety who lived on the island now called Eilean Fhianain (or Fhionnan) in lower Loch Shiel, gave his name to the village of Glenfinnan and the glen to the north of it down which the River Finnan flows into

71

Loch Shiel. His name and deeds are now known to few; but many people, Jacobite sympathizers or not, come here and are emotionally stirred by the thoughts of the name and deeds of another man, Prince Charles Edward Stuart. The walk we are suggesting here has to do with Bonnie Prince Charlie, and not with a pious monk or rock-throwing giants.

Glenfinnan lies surrounded by green fields at the head of Loch Shiel, on the A830(T) from Fort William, and is also served by the railway line from Fort William to Mallaig.

Bonnie Prince Charlie reached Glenfinnan by rowing a boat up Loch Shiel, and stepped ashore on 19 August 1745. Later that day, the royal standard was raised and Prince Charles' father, James, the Old Pretender, was proclaimed king of Scotland and Great Britain. The clansmen assembled round the standard, waved their bonnets, cheered and shouted 'Long Live King James VIII and Charles, Prince of Wales'. The Rising of '45 had begun.

The famous monument at the head of Loch Shiel, surmounted by a Highlander, commemorates this event and the men who fought and died for Prince Charles Edward Stuart.

Loch Shiel.

The walk starts a few yards behind the monument, at the National Trust for Scotland's excellent information centre which has toilet and refreshment facilities as well as a shop, bookstall and displays tracing the events of the '45 rebellion.

Just to the west of the information centre, a track turns up north from the A830(T). Follow this for just over a quarter of a mile and you will come to the fine stone viaduct which carries the railway line over Glen Finnan and the river. The track ends here, but a path carries on up under the viaduct and up the western side of the glen, with the River Finnan tumbling over its stony bed on your right.

The path follows the River Finnan for nearly three-and-a-quarter miles before petering out, and makes a splendid introduction to the wanderings of Prince Charles Stuart after his defeat at Culloden. He himself walked down this treeless, grassy glen, surrounded by high hills, in July 1746. Like you, he will have heard in the silence of this quiet glen the wind sighing in the grass and the river chattering over its bed. Unlike you – we hope – he was assailed by midges, lice and hunger.

In many places the path crosses the beds of small burns coming down from the hills, and the walk is reasonably strenuous without being arduous.

11. THE GOOSE PRINCESS
Loch Sunart

The scenery of Loch Sunart ranks among the most attractive of the Western Highlands. It is wild and lonely, yet the Isle of Mull and the resort of Oban are only a few miles away as the crow flies. By road, however, the distance is considerable as the only entry to the loch is from Loch Linnhe or by ferry from Mull and then across the Morvern peninsula. Strontian is at the head of the loch and from here the road follows the shore of the loch westward to Salen. Both villages are very small and undeveloped, though there is a hotel at Strontian.

Between the two villages, the road provides some lovely views of the loch as it winds around the spurs of hills and in and out of woods on the shore. On the way it passes Beinn Resipol (2774 feet) on the slopes of which are the old mines from which lead ores have been mined since the early eighteenth century. The element strontium is extracted from strontianite, one of the minerals found here.

At Salen the main road goes north to Acharacle on Loch Shiel and a secondary road continues west along the Ardnamurchan peninsula, the point of which is the most westerly land in mainland Britain.

This lonely and beautiful part of Scotland is the scene of one of the most touching of Scottish legends. Like many universally popular legends, including 'Swan Lake' and 'The Sleeping Beauty', it deals with the revenge of a witch for an imagined slight by a king.

According to the story told around Loch Sunart, the king and queen were well aware of the witch's evil intentions and did everything they could to protect their daughter, the object of the witch's vengeance, never

74

allowing her outside their castle unless accompanied by men-at-arms. As the girl grew up, she naturally fretted at the limits set on her freedom and developed a strong desire to escape alone from the confines of the castle, if only for a few hours. She was a romantic girl and, having fallen in love with a prince, she liked to wander by the lochside dreaming of her lover.

One beautiful spring day the urge to wander off on her own among the woods by the loch was so strong that it overruled the caution inspired by her parents' constant warnings. She strolled off along the track that followed the loch shore and, after walking some way from the castle, sat down on a fallen tree trunk where she remained deep in thought. The waters of the loch reflected the surrounding trees which were just beginning to put out the first tender green buds of spring, and the geese and swans that inhabited the lake and whom she often fed swam to and fro in front of her. Lost in her daydreams, the princess was unaware of the old witch, who had crept out of the woods and now stood behind her. The old woman began a whispered incantation as she slowly drew a circle in the sand about her feet.

As soon as the residents of the castle realized that the young princess was missing, they began to search for her, led by her lover who rode around the loch until nightfall and was up again at dawn in his frantic efforts to find her. For days they searched, and every day that went by increased their fear that the princess had been killed and perhaps disposed of in the loch.

The distraught prince took to wandering day and night around the countryside talking to everyone he found on his way and searching for a clue to the princess's disappearance. He no longer returned to the castle to sleep or to eat but spent the nights in caves or under trees, and hunted for wild fowl which he roasted over the fires he built to protect himself from wolves and other marauding animals.

One evening, as he was looking out for a wild duck or grouse for his evening meal, he saw a flight of geese moving towards him. Snatching up his bow and an arrow, he took rapid aim and fired the arrow at the breast of one of the geese. He was a good marksman and the bird plummeted to earth at his feet with the arrow transfixing its heart. As he knelt over his victim, the satisfaction of the successful hunter was tinged with a slight regret at having killed such a beautiful creature. Then his feelings turned to dreadful horror, for the grey goose was being transformed before his eyes into a slim young girl whom he recognized instantly as his princess.

Desperately, the prince tried every means he could think of to bring his sweetheart back to life, but it was no use. She was dead – killed by him and there was nothing he could do but follow her to whatever other world she had gone to.

The dead prince and princess lay hand-in-hand on the grass, their sightless eyes staring at the sky, oblivious to the cries of the geese above them. Then something strange happened. The princess gradually vanished and in her place the greylag goose appeared once more, but this goose was alive. As it struggled to rise to its feet, it cried out and then running quickly to the edge of the loch it skimmed across the water and joined the other geese that circled in the air above the prince.

THE WALK:
THE STRONTIAN GLEN
NATURE TRAIL.

MAP SQUARE:
Ordnance Survey Sheet
40/824633
More than just a stroll, this well-planned trail is through forest and across moorland. The full walk is 7 miles long, with a shortened, 4-mile walk also indicated.

Loch Sunart lies almost parallel to the Sound of Mull and converges with it at its western end. The Loch can be reached by road from the Isle of Mull by taking the ferry from Tobermory to Kilchoan on the western end of the Ardnamurchan peninsula and then continuing to Loch Sunart by car or the local bus service. From the east, the approach is via the Corran ferry south of Fort William. The ferry crosses to Argour from where the A861 leads to Strontian and Salen. There is a Shiel bus service from Argour. From the north, the approach is via Lochaillort on the A830, the 'Road to the Isles'. The railway to Mallaig (for the Skye ferry) has a station at Lochaillort.

The SUGGESTED WALK in this countryside is a nature trail that has been carefully planned by the Forestry Commission and the Nature Conservancy Council. It is the Strontian Glen Guided Walk, in the glen of the Strontian river, which flows into Loch Sunart at Strontian.

The nature reserve in which the walk is laid out lies just over a mile north of Strontian, at a right-hand turn off the road to Bellsgrove and Polloch. Just past the turn-off is a car park and picnic site. The walk begins at the car park and is well marked. It takes the visitor through quiet forests of oak, Scots pine, birch, rowan and beech and across open moorland on which sheep contentedly graze.

Both the shortened walk and the full distance offer good views of the higher peaks at the head of the Strontian Glen, of which Sgurr Dhomhnuill rises to 2914 feet, and of the clear, swift-flowing Strontian river. By the main path may also be seen charcoal rings which are relics of the seventeenth-century iron-smelting industry.

It is only on the full seven-mile walk that you will see the remains of the eighteenth-century mining settlement where the mineral strontianite was first discovered. This part of the walk takes a left fork from the main path about a mile and three-quarters from its start. It heads north to the mines then circles east and south again, following the line of a deep wooded gorge and passing a deserted croft which is still used by the sheep farm, until it rejoins the main path.

Because of the nature of the ground, you will probably not do the full seven-mile walk in much under four hours, and you will need good, stout walking shoes.

SKYE

The Faery Flag of Dunvegan
Iain Dubh
The Ghost of Duntulm Castle

12. THE FAERY FLAG OF DUNVEGAN
Dunvegan Castle

Dunvegan Castle on the Isle of Skye, home of the Chief of MacLeod, has been occupied by the MacLeods for seven centuries. The present castle, standing on a rocky outcrop on Loch Dunvegan, was built four hundred years ago. Unlike many other Highland castles, it is still lived in, is in good condition and has not suffered the depredations of war that have turned so many other headquarters of the Highland clans into crumbling ruins.

Curiously enough, the MacLeods never received deeds for the possession of their lands though they can trace their ancestry back to Olaf the Black who gave his son Leod land in the island of Lewis in the eleventh century. Leod passed the lands to his son Torquil who founded the dynasty of the MacLeods in Lewis while his other son Tormod acquired the lands on Skye by marriage. Dunvegan is therefore the seat of these Tormod MacLeods.

Having no deeds to show their rights to their lands, the MacLeods, like many other Scottish clans, had to defend them by force of arms against the aggression of the Stewarts and the MacDonalds. Their survival was due in large part to their eighth chief Alasdair Crotach (Hump Back) who obtained a charter to the lands and built the present castle. The building one sees today is the same square grey keep built by Alasdair. Though its interior has been modernized, the nine-feet-thick walls and the dungeon under the guardroom are potent reminders that this was a fortress designed to keep out enemies.

According to legend, the MacLeods have been protected by something even more powerful than their castle and their own fighting strength. Among their treasured possessions, the family still holds the object which has ensured their survival: the Faery Flag, a tattered yellow silk banner that is preserved in the castle and which is said to have supernatural powers. Its possessors knew they could wave it in three kinds of emergency to call for help, but if it were misused, then disaster would befall the MacLeods. It is said to have twice saved MacLeods, once in battle and once when a MacLeod child was on the point of death. Some say it was also waved once, for a trivial reason, by a servant in 1799, and many misfortunes fell on the family afterwards.

There are several versions of the story of how the flag, the design and style of which suggest it is of Eastern origin, came into the possession of the MacLeods. One of the more rational says that it was taken from Harold Hadrada when he was defeated by Harold of England in 1066. A more romantic version, which also helps to explain its magic quality, says that one of the MacLeods had an affair with a fairy being and that the flag was a present from her to remind him of their liaison.

The more universally accepted story of the circumstances in which the flag arrived at Dunvegan, however, is the one that follows.

William, the fourth Chief of the MacLeods, had planned a great celebration at Dunvegan Castle. All his kinsfolk and friends from far and wide were to gather there and for days before the event the servants, cooks and women of the castle were hard at work preparing food and drink for the occasion. Musicians practised their pieces, and wood was gathered for the fires in the great hall.

On the day of the celebration, MacLeod ordered one of the nurses to take the infant heir to the MacLeod lands up to a room high in the keep where he would not be disturbed by the noise of the revelry. He impressed on the woman that she was to stay by the baby's side, watching over him as he slept. The nurse promised to do so but as the sound of the celebrations floated up to her in her lonely room she was tempted to go down to watch the dancers, listen to the music and perhaps eat some of the food and drink that everyone else was enjoying.

Distracted by all the excitement, the nurse lost track of time and when she suddenly remembered her charge it was long past midnight. Anxiously, the woman ran up the stairs to the room where she had left the baby asleep and, opening the door cautiously so as not to wake him, she peered in. To her surprise and consternation she saw another woman sitting by the sleeping child. Thinking that this might be one of the other servants, she was about to whisper a question when the creature suddenly vanished.

Now thoroughly frightened, the nurse approached the cot and was relieved to find that the baby was still asleep and quite unharmed. Still alarmed, the woman picked the child up, wrapping him in a yellow silk banner that was draped over the cot. She carried him down to the Chief of the MacLeods to whom she confessed her lapse of duty. Everyone crowded around to listen to her strange story. As she told it, a silence fell over the room. MacLeod picked up his heir, fingering the silk banner and pointing out the red elfin spots with which it was decorated. He knew the significance of the faery visitation and he passed this on to his descendants with a warning that misuse of the faery powers of the flag could bring harm instead of protection to the family. The MacLeods have used it as sparingly as they were admonished to do, unfurling it in battle only when defeat was imminent and spreading it over a bed when there seemed no hope of procreating a male heir.

THE WALKS:

1. FROM DUNVEGAN CASTLE NORTH ALONG LOCH DUNVEGAN.

MAP SQUARE:

1. Ordnance Survey Sheet 23/247491

2. FROM COLBOST TO
   BORRERAIG AND
   DUNVEGAN HEAD.

2. Ordnance Survey Sheet
   23/212494
Two lochside walks.

Dunvegan lies at the north-west corner of Skye on a point of the Vaternish peninsula on the shore of Loch Dunvegan. This is a wild and rocky area with splendid coastal scenery contrasting with wooded valleys and green fields inland where a few crofters still live on the land.

Along the loch to the north there are coral beaches. Further north still, on Ardmore Bay near the northern point of Vaternish, is Trumpan, where the Faery Flag was unfurled in 1578 in a battle against pillaging MacDonalds, who had just burned to death a whole congregation inside Trumpan Church. The enraged MacLeods, helped by the Flag, left few MacDonalds alive to tell the tale.

Two main roads reach Dunvegan from southern Skye. The A850 follows the eastern side of Skye from Sligachan through

Dunvegan Castle.

Portree, and then turns west to skirt Loch Snizort Beag and Loch Greshornish before cutting across the Vaternish peninsula to Dunvegan. The west coast road is the A863, via Sligachan and the Cuillins.

There are pleasant walks in this land of the MacLeods to be enjoyed along both sides of Loch Dunvegan.

The FIRST SUGGESTED WALK here starts from the grounds of Dunvegan Castle, which is open to visitors daily except Sundays from Easter to mid-October and is well worth a visit as both castle and grounds are full of interesting things. Leave the Castle by the minor road which meets up with the A850 at the point where it, too, becomes a minor road. You are now by the loch looking across to Gairbh Eilein and ahead of you is a pleasant walk along the minor road to Claigan, two and a half miles to the north. The road is slightly inland from the shore, and skirts two small lochs and hills to the west. Almost directly opposite Claigan on the opposite shore of the loch lies Borreraig, where once flourished the famous MacCrimmon School of Piping.

The SECOND SUGGESTED WALK near Dunvegan starts at Colbost, on the B884, on the opposite side of Loch Dunvegan from the Castle, and has as its main objects the School of Piping memorial at Borreraig and Dunvegan Head, which is about five miles from Colbost. You may not want to walk the full distance here, but the scenery all round is splendid, and includes the island-dotted head of the loch to the east of Colbost, and the two flat-topped hills, Healaval Bheag and Healaval Mhor, which are known as MacLeod's Tables, south of the village.

13.   IAIN DUBH
Dunvegan Castle

There are many stories of the lawlessness and violence of
Highland chieftains who felt themselves threatened by the
ambitions of others or who themselves coveted the lands of
their neighbours. Often these quarrels were the product of
claims to succession, in some cases – as in that of Iain Dubh
– by an illegitimate elder son.

Iain Dubh – who well deserved his nickname 'black' –
was the bastard son of John, the ninth chief of the
MacLeods whose only legitimate heir was his daughter
Mary. Iain felt, perhaps rightly, that the chieftainship
should pass to him on the death of his father but since there
seemed little chance that either the chief or the clan would
nominate him, he began to think about taking by force
what was being denied him as a right. When the ninth chief
died, Iain Dubh was ready to take matters into his own
ruthless hands. After a brief lying-in-state, the body of
John MacLeod was taken from Dunvegan Castle for
burial, accompanied by his kinsmen among whom were
Mary together with two brothers and three nephews of the
dead chief, all of whom had accepted that the chief's
daughter should now be the head of the Clan MacLeod.

Iain Dubh made an excuse and did not accompany the
funeral cortège. Instead, he called together some men who
were loyal to him and prepared to take possession of the
castle. He subdued all those left behind, putting his own
men in their place, and then set a trap into which the
mourners would walk on their return. Suspecting nothing,
the funeral party crossed the drawbridge into the castle.
No sooner were they within its walls than the brothers and
nephews were seized and instantly despatched. Their

bodies were thrown with the rest of the party into the deep dungeon dug into the rock on which the castle stood. The dungeon still exists today under the guardroom floor.

By this villainous act, Iain Dubh had hoped to eliminate at one blow all those who might challenge his right to the chieftainship. He hesitated, however, at the murder of his half-sister Mary, and perhaps this was his mistake for Mary's guardian was the powerful Argyll, Chief of the Campbells, who soon became anxious at the fate of his ward.

Iain Dubh wanted to avoid a confrontation on the battlefield with the superior Argyll forces so he decided once again on a ruthless strategy. He would dispose of all or most of the Campbell chieftains at one swoop. Feigning a desire to discuss the matter of the succession to Dunvegan with the Campbell clan, he issued an invitation to all the clan heads to meet him at a banquet at Dunvegan. Eleven of the Campbell chiefs accepted, either not suspecting that there would be any foul play, or confident that their numbers would protect them.

Iain Dubh received them in a friendly fashion and appeared to agree to all the terms that the Campbells laid down. Lulled into a false sense of security, the Campbells sat down to the banquet to conclude the negotiations. Goblets were passed round to drink a toast to the happy outcome of the discussions, but as they raised them to their lips, the Campbells realized with horror that it was not wine but blood that filled them. Before they could cry out Iain Dubh's men were plunging their dirks into the terrified Campbells, who died where they sat.

Despite this appalling savagery, Iain Dubh held on to Dunvegan Castle and its estates for another three years, apparently keeping the funeral-party mourners locked up as hostages, before he was ousted by another MacLeod, aided by avenging Campbells.

THE WALK:
ON THE SOUTH-EASTERN
EDGE OF THE DURNISH
PENINSULA, FROM
ORBOST TO IDRIGILL
POINT AND MACLEOD'S
MAIDENS.

MAP SQUARE:
Ordnance Survey Sheet
23/256434
A 5-mile walk with superb
views.

*Since we have already suggested two walks near Dunvegan
Castle, we are going a little further afield this time, for a walk
to MacLeod's Maidens, three rock stacks which take their
names from yet another violent MacLeod action.*

*To reach Orbost, which lies above Loch Bharcasaig at the
north-western head of Loch Bracadale, take the B884 which
leaves the A850 at Lonmore, about a mile-and-a-half south of
Dunvegan village, and turn off it on to the Orbost road.*

*From Orbost, there is a coastal track down to Idrigill Point,
the southernmost point of Durnish. It is a splendid walk of
about five miles, offering superb views over Loch Bracadale,
of cliffs and rock-strewn coast, of caves and natural sea
arches.*

*MacLeod's Maidens are three basalt columns, the tallest of
which is 200 feet high. They rise sheer out of the sea and have
as their backdrop cliffs up to 700 feet high.*

*MacLeod's Maidens take their name from three MacLeod
women, the wife and two daughters of John, the third Chief of
the MacLeods, who were drowned when their boat was
wrecked on the rocks. Their death was caused by John's ill
temper. He had been hunting stags on the island of Harris, and
had ordered the death of a huntsman who had dared to shoot a
stag he had marked for himself. The huntsman's relatives
had, in turn, killed John just as he was stepping into his boat to
be taken home to Dunvegan. In the tumult which followed, the
boat with Chief John's family on board, slipped its moorings
and drifted off over the sea, to finish up on the Maidens.*

14. THE GHOST OF DUNTULM CASTLE
Isle of Skye

Duntulm Castle.

Duntulm Castle stands on a small rocky peninsula jutting
out between Tulm and Score bays atop a cliff against
which the waters of the Atlantic, rolling up the Little
Minch Channel between Skye and the other islands of the
Hebrides, break in a foamy ribbon. The castle, now a bleak
and sparse ruin, was probably built by the Norsemen.
Later, it was lived in by the MacLeods and then by the
MacDonalds but after the failure of the Highland Rising in
1715 it was abandoned and gradually fell into ruin.

North of the castle, the cliffs continue to Rubha Hunish,
the most northerly point of Skye; to the south the road goes

between an escarpment and the sea to Uig, embarkation port for the Hebrides.

This is a wild and desolate countryside, appropriate to legends of horror and violence. Not surprisingly, Duntulm Castle has at least one ghost that haunts the scene of his earthly misfortunes.

The MacDonald Lords of the Isles lived in Duntulm Castle. One of them had a ward, Margaret, whom he loved with a fatherly devotion, so much so that he was determined that she should marry one of his heirs. The heirs were two young men, the first a handsome youth who was the Lord of the Isles' own son and the other a cousin, equally handsome but to Margaret much more attractive for he had a dashing and romantic nature.

The Lord of the Isles naturally favoured his own son, but he was an open-minded man and was prepared to accept that Margaret might prefer the other youth. There was no urgency in bringing about a betrothal, however, for Margaret and the heirs were all young and the Lord of the Isles was still vigorous and in good health and not yet ready to relinquish his power.

The young men knew what was in the Lord of the Isles' mind and the son, who felt certain of following in his father's footsteps, was not at all impatient at waiting for the outcome of the situation. Not so his young cousin, however, who fretted at the delay and at the possibility that he would end up with neither property nor bride. Being an active and impulsive youth, the cousin felt a growing desire to take matters into his own hands and resolve the uncertainty about his future. He, therefore, began plotting with others in the castle, offering them inducements to join him in seizing it from the Lord of the Isles.

Inevitably, the young cousin's plot began to be whispered about by the conspirators. One of them, fearing that details of the plot would come to their master's ears before any action could be taken, and hoping to ingratiate himself with the Lord of the Isles, decided to betray his companions.

The Lord of the Isles found it difficult to believe that one of his own heirs, a youth whom he had brought up with the same consideration he had shown his own son, should be plotting against him, but having been convinced, his anger began to grow and he had the young man seized and put in the castle's dungeons.

He kept him there for days while he meditated on what he should do to punish the youth and, as often happens in such circumstances, during this period of suspense rumours began to fly about the castle. Conversations whispered in corners included all the gossip that the inhabitants of the castle knew about Margaret and the cousin. When the Lord of the Isles learnt that his ward had favoured the cousin and not his own son, the motives for the plot began to be revealed – or so he thought.

Now the Lord of the Isles determined that the punishment would have to include both young people and as he lay awake at night he thought up a diabolical scheme.

Next day, he gave orders to his servants to tie up the young prisoner and to seat him in an alcove in the dungeon with a jug of water and an empty plate. Having done that, they were to start bricking up the alcove, leaving a gap through which they could cut the young man's bonds before completing the job of sealing him in.

After the gruesome work was completed, the Lord of the Isles swore to secrecy all those who knew about it and the life of the castle continued as if nothing had happened. Margaret knew, of course, that the muffled sounds and screams she could hear coming from the dungeon had to be from her cousin, but everyone feigned ignorance of them, including the Lord of the Isles who told her that she was suffering from an overwrought imagination. Finally, the noises ceased and Margaret, once a pretty girl, became haggard and unkempt and her mind seemed to have lost its ability to concentrate on the simplest things. She had no appetite for food or for life itself, and she pined away and eventually died. Her spirit could not tear itself away from the spot where her love was entombed, and it haunts the castle still. According to some, the sounds you hear if you stand quietly by the ruins are not the pounding of the surf and the cry of seagulls, but the beating of fists against a wall and the weeping of a distressed girl.

THE WALK:	MAP SQUARE:
AN EASY WALK FROM	Ordnance Survey Sheet
DUNTULM CASTLE TO	23/409743
KILMUIR.	This walk is along a main road, so is not really suitable for very young children.

Duntulm Castle lies at the northern end of the Trotternish peninsula of Skye, which is reached from mainland Scotland via two ferry routes. The main one is between Kyle of Lochalsh in Western Ross and Kyleakin on Skye, the stretch of water between the two ferry points being only a few hundred yards wide. Kyle of Lochalsh lies at the end of the A87 from Fort William, and is also a rail terminal. The other ferry route is through Glenelg and across to Kylerhea (summer only).

Once on Skye, you can drive to Duntulm via the A850 to Portree, then the A855 to Duntulm. There is a bus service from Portree to Kilmaluag (the Duntulm Hotel).

When you have viewed what little remains of Duntulm Castle, there is an easy walk south which should awaken memories of another romantic story in Scotland's history – Flora MacDonald's part in the escape of Bonnie Prince Charlie from Scotland after the '45 rising.

For this walk, follow the A855 south from Duntulm in the direction of Uig. After a little under two miles, you will come to the Kilmuir cemetery on the left-hand side of the road; here

Flora MacDonald is buried. A little off the main road, up the left-hand turning you will come to after the cemetery, is the monument to Flora Macdonald, standing on a hillside looking over coast and sea. The memorial is in the shape of a Celtic cross.

It is a good point at which to pause and ponder on the bravery of this young girl who, despite the danger, agreed to help Bonnie Prince Charlie escape from the small Hebridean island of Benbecula. She had to obtain a military passport to allow her and her 'Irish spinning maid' named 'Betty Burke' to cross over to Skye, ostensibly so that Flora could visit her mother. 'Betty Burke' was, of course, the Prince in disguise, and they had to run the gauntlet both of very rough seas and, once they had reached Skye, of military patrols on the coast before they reached a safe haven.

Flora was arrested on suspicion of having aided the Prince, and spent some time in the Tower of London. She eventually came back to Skye, married, and had a large family. She spent some time in America before returning to die at a good old age.

Before retracing your walk to Duntulm, visit the Kilmuir Croft Museum where the exhibition of domestic and agricultural utensils and implements gives a good idea of what life was like for the crofters of a century and more ago. The museum is open on weekdays from Easter to October.

THE GREAT GLEN

The Loch Ness Monster
The Well of the Seven Heads
Ailean nan Creach and the Cats

15. THE LOCH NESS MONSTER
Loch Ness

The Great Glen that cuts through Scotland is a rift valley containing a string of lochs, rivers and canals that provide a means of water communication across Scotland between the North and Irish Seas. Of all the stretches of water that lie in the glen the largest is Loch Ness. At its northern end it reaches to within a few miles of Inverness, a fine market town through which the River Ness carries the waters of Loch Ness to the sea. Twenty-four miles away lies Loch Ness's southern end – at Fort Augustus, a pleasant town built in 1715. The site of the fort is now a Benedictine abbey and school whose fine modern church and museum can be visited.

Halfway along Loch Ness, at its widest point, is Castle Urquhart, a picturesque ruin built on a stony crag by the edge of the loch's western shore. The main road down the Great Glen, the A82, runs along the west side of Loch Ness and offers a series of good views as it winds its way through the trees by the water's edge. On the eastern shore of the loch, a secondary road from Fort Augustus joins the loch at Foyers and then becomes the A862 to Inverness at Dores.

Loch Ness has a dark and brooding look even in fine weather, due in part to the gloomy coniferous forest that blankets its eastern side, and its great depth, which reaches 700 feet in places. This sombre appearance has undoubtedly had something to do with the growth of the belief that a monster lives in Loch Ness, though it seems that monsters are not unusual in the Great Glen, for another legendary monster also inhabits Loch Oich.

Though the monster has reached its greatest fame in our time, thanks to the efforts of the mass media, it has been known for centuries. It was already something of a celebrity in the days of St Columba, in the sixth century, for in a book on the life of the saint there is an account of the beast's being frightened away from an intended victim by the holy man who called on it to go away in God's name. This suggests that Nessie has mellowed over the years; today's monster is supposed to be a shy and peaceful creature, and keeps well away from human beings – which is why he, or she, is so difficult to photograph.

There have been many sightings of the monster over a long period of time. It has even been photographed, though hazily, but final and conclusive proof of its existence is always lacking, despite well-publicized expeditions by American and other scientists, equipped with diving gear and underwater cameras and ready to spend weeks on the loch, if necessary, in their hunt for Nessie. Maybe she – or he – sees them coming and lies low till they have gone.

Thus the sceptical see no reason to suspend their disbelief, though many others, including many serious and scientifically minded people, are convinced that some kind of extraordinary creature does indeed exist under the waters of the loch. A popular site for the monster's den is in the waters under Castle Urquhart.

Descriptions of the monster vary, some people swearing to a creature with the appearance of a camel, others to one resembling a snake. The most widely accepted description is that it has a large body, long neck and small head, not unlike a plesiosaur from the age of the dinosaurs.

One thing is certain – until there is proof one way or the other, the monster legend, like those about flying saucers, is here to stay. On the one hand it provides the loch with revenue from tourists and on the other a continuing field of study for romantically minded scientists.

The visitor will find plenty of information about the Loch Ness monster at the Great Glen Exhibition in Fort

Augustus (open June to September, Monday to Saturday 10.00–18.00, Sunday 14.00–18.00), and at the new Loch Ness Monster Exhibition beside the Drumnadrochit Hotel on the A82 a mile from Castle Urquhart (open daily).

Castle Urquhart.

THE WALK:
FROM CASTLE URQUHART TO UPPER LENIE, ON THE HILLS ABOVE LOCH NESS.

MAP SQUARE:
Ordnance Survey Sheet 26/532286
This walk, starting and finishing at Castle Urquhart, is about 5 miles long but can be halved if you drive from the castle over Borlum Bridge, where there is a car park by the Lewiston Arms. You then walk back over the bridge to the Bunloit Road.

Castle Urquhart stands on a promontory called Strone Point on the north-western shore of Loch Ness by the village of

Strone. It is a very impressive ruin indeed, silhouetted against the waters of the loch and the hills of the far shore. The castle was given by James IV to James Grant of Freuchie in 1509, and was blown up in 1692 to prevent the Jacobites occupying it. The castle can be visited, and is open every day (afternoons only on Sundays).

The walk starts at the castle, from where most of the 'sightings' of the monster have been made. Once you have spent a few minutes looking for Nessie, return to the A82(T) and walk in the direction of Strone and Drumnadrochit (that is, in the direction of Inverness). You will walk through Strone and the tiny village of Borlum and then, a mile and a quarter from the start of the walk, you will reach Borlum Bridge over the River Coiltie. Turn left before the bridge on to the minor road to Bunloit. Once through what looks like a dumping ground for building materials, you will find that this narrow metalled road becomes very picturesque. It offers fine views of the valley behind Lewiston.

Much of the walk is steep, with numerous hairpin bends, edged with stone walls, near the beginning, so it is quite strenuous walking. The Forestry Commission's Borlum Forest is on your left as you walk up. Just under a mile and a quarter from Borlum Bridge, you will come to Woodend, where the larches and pines of the forest give way to scrubland. Past Woodend, the first gate on the left, marked 'Private', is a forest track leading to the historic little hamlet of Upper Lenie, where you should have some good views of Loch Ness.

16. THE WELL OF THE SEVEN HEADS
Loch Oich

If you are driving down the Great Glen along the main road, the A82(T) which skirts all three lochs in the Glen, you will pass towards the southern end of Loch Oich (the

Monument of the Well of the Seven Heads, Loch Oich.

middle one of the three) a strange monument. It stands on the edge of the loch's western shore, two miles south of Invergarry just by the road, and it is well worth stopping to have a look at, for it commemorates an incredibly blood-stained story of Highland vengeance.

The monument of the Well of the Seven Heads is an obelisk sitting on a square plinth. Topping the obelisk are seven bearded heads, and on the four sides of the plinth its story of 'ample and summary vengeance' is told in Gaelic, English, Latin and French. The monument was erected in 1812 by Colonel Alister Ranaldson MacDonell of Glengarry in memory of an incident which had occurred in his family 300 years before (according to the monument; historically, 1663 seems the more correct date for the incident).

MacDonell, eleventh Chief of Keppoch, a cadet branch of the Macdonnells of Glengarry, had two young sons whom he wished to see grow into cultured and cultivated young men, well educated and socially polished. The Scottish connection with France still being strong, he sent young Alasdair and his brother to that country to be educated.

While his heirs were away, MacDonell of Keppoch drew seven kinsmen, possibly his brothers, into the management of the estate. The seven found the work to their liking, and grew to regard the Keppoch properties as their own. After all, the decisions and actions which had made the land fertile and prosperous had been theirs, not those of two probably over-educated and soft young lads learning effete ways in France.

Then MacDonell of Keppoch died suddenly and, after an interval of some months, his two sons came home from France to claim their inheritance. Their seven uncles viewed their arrival with a jealous dislike and very soon murdered Alasdair MacDonell, twelfth Chief of Keppoch, and his brother.

The uncles' enjoyment of their ill-gotten estate was short-lived, however. Keppoch's kinsman, the bard Iain Lom MacDonell, he of the honest heart and persuasive tongue, was roused to bitter fury at the young laird's murder and that of his brother. Having failed to persuade the Glengarry chief, Lord MacDonell and Aros, to avenge the deaths, he won help from Sir John Macdonald of Sleat, and the seven brothers were killed – a demonstration of the 'swift course of feudal justice' (to quote the words on the monument) which needed no courts or lawyers to give it effect.

The victims' heads were chopped off, and their bodies buried. (The writer, Hamish MacInnes, records that quite recently the bodies of seven men were dug up in Glen Spean, complete but for their heads.) Iain Lom took the ghastly bleeding heads and washed them in the spring called Tobar nan Ceann, which flows into Loch Oich near its southern end. The spring is still there, beneath the monument, though the road has been built over it. Then the poet took the heads and presented them to Lord MacDonell of Glengarry at his stronghold, Invergarry Castle on the shore of Loch Oich, as a gruesome reminder of what Iain Lom considered Glengarry's obligations to his kinsmen to be.

What happened to these grisly trophies no one knows. If the heads were kept at Invergarry Castle, then they did not survive the destruction of the castle at the hands of Cumberland's troops after the '45 rising. Invergarry was marked for destruction simply because Bonnie Prince Charlie had slept there before and after Culloden – another example of 'summary vengeance' in Scottish history.

THE WALKS:
1. TWO WALKS IN THE
   FORESTRY
   COMMISSION'S
   GLENGARRY FOREST.

MAP SQUARE:
1. Ordnance Survey Sheet
   34/283013

2. A VERY SHORT WALK
TO INVERGARRY
CASTLE.

2. Ordnance Survey Sheet
34/317010
Walk one is 1½ or 2 miles
long. Walk two is a stroll at
will.

*Glen Garry is one of several beautiful glens which run west
from the Great Glen, and is a main route to the Kyle of
Lochalsh and Skye. Its floor is filled by the long sheet of
water which is Loch Garry, and with the River Garry flowing
through it to join Loch Oich at Invergarry, the Glen is a
splendid panorama of water, hill and forest. No wonder the
seven brothers of MacDonell of Keppoch coveted the country
enough to commit murder for it.*

*Our FIRST SUGGESTED WALK makes use of the
paths laid out by the Forestry Commission in their Glengarry
Forest, south of Loch Garry. Coming from the Great Glen,
you turn west off the A82(T) at Invergarry, on to the A87(T),
the Kyle of Lochalsh road.*

*Two miles along the A87(T) you will see the entrance to the
Forest sign-posted on your left. (Don't be side-tracked by the
notice indicating the Forestry Commission's offices on your
right a few hundred yards before this.) A few hundred yards
along the track from the entrance gates, the Forestry
Commission have provided a car park and a pretty woodland
picnic site on the edge of a stream.*

*Within the Forest, two walks have been laid out, both
starting from the picnic place. The walks, one of which is a
mile and a half long, the other two miles, both have as their
climax a spectacular waterfall. One walk follows a stream
and the other, after a steep climb near its beginning,
approaches the falls from above before dropping back down to
a footbridge. The paths are both well marked and sign-posts
alert you to points of interest to watch out for.*

*Our SECOND SUGGESTED WALK really should not
be here, for it is no more than a stroll in a garden, but it does*

Glen Garry.

have as its object the splendid ruin of Invergarry Castle, and so is worth mentioning.

The garden in question is that of the delightful Glengarry Castle Hotel, once a private Victorian mansion, sitting on a terrace and surrounded by a garden of lawns, flower beds and shrubberies stretching to the edge of Loch Oich.

The hotel is eight miles south of Fort Augustus on the A82(T) and is well sign-posted. Its garden is reached by a small gate in the hedge to the right of the main entrance, and you see the ruins of the castle appearing through the trees away to your right.

Should it be out of season and the hotel closed when you visit, Invergarry Castle may also be reached by a track forking off the A82(T) half a mile south of the bridge over the River Garry.

The castle is a typical Scottish tower, built with great square-cut stones said to have been brought to the site on the backs of clansmen from more than seven miles away. The ruins are extensive enough for you to imagine what the castle must have been like at the time of its occupation. Probably very little of this building dates from the time of the Well of the Seven Heads incident, as the castle was rebuilt not long before Prince Charles Stuart stayed there.

17. AILEAN NAN CREACH AND THE CATS
River Lochy

The River Lochy runs between Loch Lochy and Fort William on Loch Linnhe and for all its short course of nine miles it has the Caledonian Canal running alongside or near it. This western end of the Great Glen is brimming with interest and the scenery, which includes Ben Nevis, is really grand. The main road along the valley is the A82(T) from Fort William which traces the route of the old military road built by General Wade in the period between the two Jacobite risings of 1715 and 1745.

Fort William itself is today a large commercial and holiday centre whose long main street is lined with many shops, hotels and restaurants. Steamer services to Mull and Skye as well as good bus services in all directions make Fort William a good jumping-off point for excursions.

Gairlochy lock on the Caledonian Canal.

Generations before Fort William was built or even thought of, there lived in the valley of the River Lochy a man called Ailean nan Creach, a Chief of Clan Cameron who, as his name 'Alan of the Forays' suggests, was a reckless fighter and a fierce warrior. He had made at least seven forays against his enemies, and had killed many people. As he grew older, he began to meditate on the events of his life and to regret having caused so much havoc and destruction, albeit in the cause of war. He began to feel increasingly uneasy at having cut short the lives of so many, and wondered what sort of reception he would get in the next world if he left his sins unexpiated in this one.

Having no one to turn to but an old witch who lived on the banks of the River Lochy, Ailean told her his troubles and asked her what he ought to do about them.

The witch looked up her book of spells and having found something that seemed suitable for a man in Ailean nan Creach's situation, she gave him full instructions as to what he should do.

That night, Ailean gathered up a sackful of peat and grabbing his house cat, he tied him up and stuffed him into it, then set off for the slopes of a nearby mountain. Having found a quiet spot where he could carry out the witch's instructions undisturbed, he emptied the sack and, leaving the cat struggling with its bonds, he began to collect some twigs and branches for firewood.

Next, Ailean cut some branches off a nearby tree and fashioned a spit on to which he tied his unfortunate cat. By this time, the animal was thoroughly alarmed and wailing in terror. Ailean did not falter in his task, despite the shrieks of an animal which had been his pet, for he was more preoccupied with his immortal soul than with the fate of his cat.

Having arranged everything to his liking Ailean, following the witch's instructions, now set fire to the pile of twigs which burnt merrily. Soon the peat began to glow and give off considerable heat. As the temperature rose, the wails of the cat changed to heart-rending screams which could he heard all along the River Lochy Valley and even further.

The screams of their fellow cat in distress attracted other cats from far and wide; black cats, grey cats and white cats, wild mountain cats and domestic cats all heard the cries carried on the wind and soon the slope where Ailean had built his fire was alive with cats, their eyes shining ominously in the dark.

Though he was a brave man, Ailean felt decidedly nervous at being surrounded by this threatening mob of feline creatures whose claws could tear him to pieces if they decided to attack. But they did not. They seemed rather to be waiting for someone. Suddenly that 'someone' appeared. It was a gigantic black cat with baleful yellow eyes who advanced on the fire and with one sweep of his paw scattered the glowing peat and the twigs over Ailean nan Creach's feet and stood glowering at him. Ailean fingered the dirk with which he had cut the branches and waited for the creature to attack.

Suddenly, to his amazement, the huge creature spoke. 'Ailean nan Creach,' it said, 'we will not kill you because you are a stupid and credulous man and you have no more thought about what you are doing to my kinsman than you thought about all the other people who have died because of your ignorance and stupidity. But we will spare you on one condition only.'

The cat then went on to tell Ailean nan Creach that he could expiate his sins far more thoroughly by doing good works than by practising witchcraft which only added to the world's mischief and to the suffering of others. It suggested to Ailean that one of the ways in which he could do good was to build seven churches – one for each of his forays – where no churches had existed before. Thus he would be bringing a good influence into the lives of people who might otherwise, like Ailean, be depending on witches to guide them.

Ailean, by now thoroughly demoralized, was ready to agree to almost anything that the giant cat demanded and he readily agreed to devote the rest of his life to the task the cat had suggested. No sooner had he said so than his smouldering victim was released and ran down the hill to the river, followed by all the other cats who jumped in the river after him and swam away, never to be seen again.

True to his word, Ailean nan Creach built churches at Loch Leven, Kildonan, Kilmallie, Kilchoan, Kill-a-choreill, Kilkellen and Morven.

THE WALK:
ALONG THE TOWPATH OF
THE CALEDONIAN CANAL
FROM GAIRLOCHY VIA
BANAVIE TO CORPACH
AND LOCH EIL.

MAP SQUARE:
Ordnance Survey Sheet
41/177842
An easy walk along a historic
stretch of canal.

This eight-mile walk traces the course of the final section of the Caledonian Canal in the valley of the River Lochy, which is in the Lochaber District at the southern end of the Great Glen. Several bus services out of Fort William serve the area, and the Glasgow–Fort William railway stops at Spean Bridge.

The walk is very pleasant, offering fine views of Ben Nevis to the south, as well as providing extra entertainment in the form of the boats, mostly fishing boats and pleasure craft, which use this historic canal.

The Caledonian Canal was engineered and built by Thomas Telford in the 1820s with government money – the only canal in Britain to be so financed. It is a ship canal and is still regularly used by inshore fishing craft. The engineering work on this section of the canal is particularly interesting. .

Begin the walk at Gairlochy at the western end of Loch Lochy, at the lock on the canal immediately below the bridge which carries the B8004 over the river, starting along the towpath on the eastern bank.

Between Gairlochy and Banavie, a stretch of nearly six miles, you will pass two sets of locks and a swing bridge. Then, at Banavie, comes the famous flight of eight locks known as Neptune's Staircase. These locks lift craft over a difference in level of some 64 feet.

Immediately below Neptune's Staircase are two swing bridges, one carrying the A830(T) and the other the West Highland Railway line. Three-quarters-of-a-mile further on come two more locks which lower the canal into the shipping basin at Corpach, two miles from Fort William. There is usually a good variety of shipping to be seen in the basin, while Corpach can offer a selection of pubs and cafés to the holidaymaker and walker.

NB: If this walk seems too long, you can shorten it considerably by crossing to the western bank at any of the locks or the swing bridge above Banavie, to return to Gairlochy.

THE SOUTH-WESTERN HIGHLANDS

The Lovers of Loch Leven

The Massacre of Glen Coe

Stewart of Appin and Ticonderoga

The Red Book of Appin

Deirdre of the Sorrows

Black Colin and his Faithful Wife

The Murdered Bridegroom

The Three-score Fools of Lorn

The Carpenter MacPheigh

18. THE LOVERS OF LOCH LEVEN
Loch Leven

At its seaward end Loch Leven is a wide loch with tree-covered hillsides sloping up to the rocky summits of Beinn a Bheithir to the south and Creag Bhreac to the north. North Ballachulish and Ballachulish face each other at the mouth of the loch where a bridge carries the A82 on over the narrows. Ballachulish itself is on the south bank of the loch on the route to Glencoe village. To the east of the hotel in Ballachulish is the spot where James Stewart of the Glens was hanged by the Campbells on suspicion that he had shot and killed the Red Fox, Colin Campbell. A monument marks the spot, which inspired Robert Louis Stevenson to write his exciting novel *Kidnapped*.

To the east, the loch narrows at Glencoe and continues between high wooded hills to where Kinlochleven, a small but not very attractive industrial community, stands at its head.

Opposite Glencoe stands Callert House, the scene of a legend of lovers long ago, though the house has been rebuilt since then.

According to the story, the master of Callert had a pretty daughter, Mairi, whom he guarded jealously for to his way of thinking there was no one along Loch Leven worthy to be her husband. However Mairi, who was a friendly and gregarious girl, had other ideas and, of course, it happened that one day she began secretly to meet a young man from Inverawe whom she encountered while he was working on Loch Leven. His name was Diarmid and he came from Loch Awe, where his parents had a mansion as fine as the one owned by the Laird of Callert. Soon, Mairi and Diarmid were deeply in love.

Loch Leven with Glen Coe in the background.

Though Mairi's father, the Laird, did not know about Diarmid's background, he was suspicious of him and forbade Mairi from going into Ballachulish to see Diarmid while he was there.

It happened one day that a trading ship arrived in the loch, a great event equal to market day, and everyone in the Callert household, except Mairi, who was shut up in her bedchamber to prevent her going, went off to the village to see what they could buy from among the splendid materials and beautiful leather goods that the ship was carrying.

Mairi was half tempted to climb out of the window of her room but since Ballachulish was a small place she knew her father would spot her, and there would only be a terrible scene so she accepted her lot though not without some grumblings of discontent and disappointment.

As it turned out, she was the lucky one, for all the other members of the house who came back laden with the spoils of their shopping expedition were taken ill overnight and were either dead or close to dying by the following morning. Mairi was unaware of this, because her father, having arrived back late at night, had not thought to unlock her door, but she was aware of the unnatural silence in the house.

Looking out of her window in the morning, she saw the plague flag flying over the ship, while from the houses in the village a band of men advanced towards the house with more flags which they placed at the entrance gate.

This told Mairi at once that all the inhabitants of the house, including her father and all the other people she had grown up with, must be dead. After she had recovered somewhat from the shock of losing all her loved ones, Mairi began to realize that there was plenty to worry about concerning her own situation. She had to watch out now for the men who would arrive to burn the house down in order to prevent the plague spreading, and to warn them somehow that she was still locked up in it.

An hour went by then another while she watched the smoke rising from the plague-stricken houses that were being fired in the village. Eventually, she saw a group of men walking along the track that led to Callert House. In their hands were the flaming torches with which they were setting fire to the brushwood along the path. When she called out to them they looked surprised and dismayed, and when she explained that she was locked in and that she had not been to the plague ship they could not hide their scepticism.

Clearly, they were at a loss to know what to do next. They had been sent to burn the house down but they could hardly do so with a pretty young girl still inside it, especially since she looked perfectly healthy. While they were deliberating what they should do Mairi called out to their leader and asked him not to do anything at all until a message had been sent to Diarmid, who had returned home to Inverawe, explaining her plight. Relieved at not having to make such a difficult decision, or at least at being able to postpone it, the leader of the men agreed to her wish and sent one of his men post haste to tell her lover.

When Diarmid heard the news he mounted his fastest horse and rode to Loch Leven, arriving just as it was getting dark. Waiting until the men who guarded the house were asleep, he threw a rope up to the window of Mairi's room and helped her to escape.

He did not know, of course, whether or not she had caught the plague too, and as a precaution he made her bathe in the loch and then put on some of his own clothes before they set off for Loch Awe and his home.

The news of the plague had been spread at Inverawe by the messenger who had come to find Diarmid, so that when they arrived the lovers received an inhospitable welcome. Even Diarmid's own father would not take them in, although he did agree that if they went away and lived on Ben Cruachan for forty days without contacting any other human being he would assume that they were both healthy and receive them again in the house. Being a Godfearing man, and a highly moral one, he blessed them before they set off and made them repeat the words of the marriage ceremony.

The forty days and nights on the mountain passed all too quickly for Mairi and Diarmid and their unusual honeymoon remained one of the happiest experiences of their lives which, like those of all legendary lovers, were long and happy.

THE WALKS:	MAP SQUARE:
1. A HILL WALK FROM CALLERT HOUSE SKIRTING MAM NA GUALAINN.	Ordnance Survey Sheet 41/093603 The elderly may find the first of these walks a strain, but

2. FROM CALLERT HOUSE
   WEST ALONG LOCH
   LEVEN.

the second walk provides
an easy alternative.

*The house now called Callert House is on the north shore of
Loch Leven and is reached from Fort William via the A82(T)
and from Oban via the A828, which links up with the A82(T)
at Ballachulish. Callert House is on the A82 about two miles
from where it turns off the A82(T) in North Ballachulish, a
pleasant drive along the wooded lochside.*

*The views across the water to Glencoe and the Glencoe
Forest are very fine, and become even more spectacular from
the path running up the hill behind Callert House, which is the
starting point for both suggested walks.*

*For the FIRST SUGGESTED WALK, follow the
driveway which starts at the main road beside Callert House,
and which traces the eastern edge of the forest which grows
across the hill here. This is a private drive, and you should
ask at the farm behind the house for permission to walk
up the hill. The path then descends across the slope of Mam na
Gualainn to Laitigmor, where it joins the Old Military Road.
A serious walker could follow this road west and north to Fort
William or east and south to the Kingshouse Hotel in Glen
Coe. However, I am suggesting that you walk just to the
northern edge of the forest.*

*This walk is barely one and a half miles, but the path is
quite steep and so is not just a gentle stroll. The effort is worth
it, however, as the scenery is a great panorama of spectacular
and romantic peaks. To the east lies Beinn na Caillach (2502
feet), with the summits of the Mamore Forest range rising
beyond. Look south-east over Loch Leven, and you will see the
entrance to Glen Coe, with several small islands in the loch in
front of it. The largest of these islands is Eilean Munde, once a
MacDonald burial place, where the ruins of the chapel may
still be seen. Beyond are the serrated ridges of Aonach Eagach
which, on its far side, falls steeply into the Pass of Glen Coe.*

The SECOND SUGGESTED WALK is for those who want just an easy stroll. From the path by Callert House, turn left along the track which runs westward parallel to the loch side for less than half a mile.

19. THE MASSACRE OF GLEN COE
Glen Coe

Even without the story of the massacre that took place under the beetling crags of the Three Sisters, the glen through which the River Coe flows from Rannoch Moor west into Loch Leven would be memorable. At the top of the glen arises the mass of Buchaille Etive Mor, a 3345-feet mass of rock which rises from the flat, boggy expanse of Rannoch Moor like a fortress to guard the descent into Glen Coe. Opposite from Altnafeadh winds a rocky track, the upper part of which is known as the Devil's Staircase, and to the west, above the Kingshouse Hotel, is Meall a Buiridh, a mountain whose slopes are dotted with colourfully dressed skiers every winter.

As you approach the glen along the A82(T) from Rannoch Moor the mountain sides press in as you approach the Pass of Glen Coe. At this point, a bluff called The Study (from an old Scots word 'stiddie' meaning 'anvil') provides a fine vantage point for the magnificent view of the sombre gorge with its great sweeping treeless slopes that lead the eye up to the precipitous sides of the Three Sisters: Beinn Fhada, Gearr Aonach and Aonach Dubh, high on the west side of which is the cave in which the great Celtic poet, Ossian, is said to have lived. In spring and winter the waterfalls drop tumultuously to the pool known as the Meeting of Three Waters. Near here, in the corrie between the two easternmost Sisters, Gearr Aonach and Beinn Fhada, the MacDonalds who lived in the glen hid and grazed the cattle they had stolen.

Further down the glen is the Glen Coe Visitor Centre run by the National Trust for Scotland, a well-appointed place with a car park, picnic facilities, snack bar and toilets, together with a well-stocked book and gift shop. Behind it lies the Clachaig Hotel.

Beyond here the road dips down towards Glencoe village which is surrounded by green wooded hills providing a pleasant contrast to the harsh, bare rock of the upper glen. Near the village at the old Bridge of Coe stands the memorial to the MacDonalds who fell to the treacherous swords of the Campbells on that bitterly cold night in February 1692.

Glen Coe.

Though Highland history is not short on bloody and murderous incident, the massacre at Glen Coe lives on as a particularly cold-blooded deed perpetrated against an unsuspecting people, its horror compounded by the fact that it broke the near-sacred law of Highland hospitality.

The massacre took place during the reign of William of Orange who, having ousted the Stuart King James II mounted the throne as William III. He then pardoned the Scots who had fought to keep a Stuart on the English and

Scottish thrones. The pardon extended only until 1 January 1692, when all the clans who had not submitted and sworn allegiance to the new king were to be considered outlaws. The MacDonalds of Glen Coe could not accept the oath without the approval of the man they considered their true king, the exiled James II, and their chief delayed going to Fort William to make his submission until the very last day of December 1691. Once there, he found there was no one to hear his oath, and he had to go on to Inveraray, which he did not reach until 2 January – one day too late.

As the oath of allegiance was not made by the day laid down, orders were given to the commander of the King's army in Scotland to set about the destruction of the MacDonald clan. A force of one hundred and twenty men from the Argyll Regiment was despatched to Glen Coe under Campbell of Glen Lyon, a man who had no reason to love the MacDonalds for their thefts of his cattle had made him poor. Campbell did not immediately attack the MacDonalds but instead assured them that the only reason for his visit was that Fort William was so overcrowded with soldiery that he had been ordered to billet his men elsewhere, and had chosen Glen Coe.

Lulled into a false sense of security, the MacDonalds went about their everyday work and gave the Argyll soldiers the best welcome they could in the MacDonald dwellings that were strung along the glen. On the night of 12 January 1692, Campbell visited Alexander MacDonald and stayed late playing cards and drinking with him. That night, snow began to fall, covering the paths and making any kind of movement difficult. The pass became blocked with snow and the pools of water turned to ice as the temperature dropped. Both soldiers and MacDonalds huddled in their blankets to keep warm. Then, at five in the morning while it was still dark, the soldiers rose quietly in order not to disturb the unsuspecting MacDonalds and at a given signal set about exterminating the entire clan; young men, old men, women and even children, all were to be murdered and their homes destroyed by fire. In the confusion and darkness many of the MacDonalds escaped up into the mountains where they now had to risk the possibility of dying from exposure. Under the circumstances, it is surprising how many did survive, for out of the 150 MacDonalds in the glen that night well over a hundred were still alive next day to see their cattle and horses being driven off to Fort William.

Inevitably the story of the Glen Coe Massacre aroused the strongest feelings and still does, for there is no doubt that it was a treacherous and bloody deed. The relatively small number of deaths does suggest, though, that perhaps the show of strength by the government did not have the full support of the soldiers, or the clan would surely have been entirely wiped out.

The survivors eventually returned to their land and their cattle-raising, feeling protected, perhaps, by the outcry that the massacre of their kinsmen had aroused throughout the country. They continued to be loyal to the Stuarts and fought for them in both the uprisings of 1715 and 1745, but theirs was a lost cause. In the end, they were swept away from their homes by the Highland Clearances of the eighteenth and early nineteenth centuries.

THE WALKS:	MAP SQUARE:
1. ALONG THE WEST HIGHLAND WAY FROM NEAR THE KINGSHOUSE HOTEL, VIA ALTNAFEADH TO THE DEVIL'S STAIRCASE.	1. Ordnance Survey Sheet 41/251550
	2. Ordnance Survey Sheet 41/128564
	3. Ordnance Survey Sheet 41/128564
2. FROM THE GLEN COE VISITOR INFORMATION CENTRE TO THE STUDY	None of these walks is a simple stroll being of varying degrees of difficulty. Proper,

AND ON TO THE
KINGSHOUSE HOTEL.

3. FROM THE GLEN COE
   VISITOR INFORMATION
   CENTRE TO SIGNAL
   ROCK.

stout walking shoes are
essential.

*Glen Coe lies on the A82(T) between Rannoch Moor in the east
and Loch Leven in the west. At Glencoe village the road turns
westward along the southern shore of the loch to its head,
providing superb views of the upper loch as it climbs along the
edge of the steep, wooded hills. At Kinlochleven, an industrial
village built round an aluminium works, the road curves back
along the north shore of Loch Leven and then up to Fort
William. Before the bridge was built to replace the ferry at
Ballachulish, this was the main road between Fort William
and Rannoch Moor. At the time of the Massacre, there was no
road through the Pass of Glencoe.*

*Loch Leven and Glen Coe provide superb country for hill
walking, popular with visitors in both summer and winter.
Much of the Glen Coe walking is for the really fit and
experienced walker, and can involve rock and ice climbing as
well as walking. The three walks described here are
considerably less ambitious but can still provide some
strenuous walking, as well as offering many breathtaking and
superb views of this magnificent country.*

*The FIRST SUGGESTED WALK follows the recently
planned West Highland Way. Its starting point is to the west
of the Kingshouse Hotel, on the minor road which runs from
the A82(T) to the hotel. A few hundred yards from the point
where you turn off the A82(T) on to the minor road, you will
see one of the new signposts indicating the West Highland
Way. At this point, the Way follows the old military road,
now a barely discernible track, running parallel to the motor
road for about two and a half miles to Altnafeadh where it
turns up past the keeper's house and through a section of wood*

up the side of Beinn Bheag. Walk on up towards the saddle between Beinn Bheag and the Stob Mhic Martuin, a distance of about a mile. As it reaches the summit ridge (1800 feet) the path zigzags steeply. This is the famous Devil's Staircase, and from here the views are superb, though those who suffer from vertigo may feel a little queasy. The energetic may continue the walk from here into Kinlochleven, a distance of about six miles, but to complete the suggested walk, retrace your steps back to the road.

The SECOND SUGGESTED walk starts at the National Trust for Scotland's Visitor Information Centre, below the Pass (open Easter to October), which has a shop, café and toilets as well as a car park. Detailed information on walks is available here. Leaving your car, turn left along the main road for about a mile and a quarter, passing Loch Achtriochtan on your right. Traditionally, a water-bull haunts this loch, so watch out for him! Just past here, there are several points where you can leave the road to pick up the grassy track which meanders along the valley floor north of the River Coe. Above and to your right tower the great bulks of the Three Sisters, with Ossian's Cave visible as a fissure in the rock high up on the most westerly of the three, Aonach Dubh.

After about one and a half miles, another track goes off to the right from the one you are walking along, crosses a footbridge over the Coe and climbs up the corrie – Coire nan Lochan – between Aonach Dubh and Gearr Aonach, the central Sister. This is a steep path for the adventurous. Less than half a mile further along the main track, a second track branches off right, crosses the Coe via a footbridge and leads up the steep ravine, Allt Coire Gabhail, between Gearr Aonach and the third Sister, Beinn Fhada. Up here, the MacDonalds kept their stolen cattle.

Keeping to the main track, you are now walking along the narrowest section of the Pass of Glencoe, and will very quickly reach the Meeting of the Waters, where several streams cascade into the River Coe. A few yards past here, the track meets the A82(T) again. Keeping to the track, cross the main road and carry on up the Pass. Just over a quarter of a mile further on, having passed a few buildings at Allt-na-reigh, you will reach the head of the gorge and The Study, one of the best-known viewpoints in Glen Coe. Even Queen Victoria picnicked here.

If you feel you have walked far enough, The Study is the ideal place to stop and admire the magnificent panorama of mountain and glen before returning to your starting point. You could carry on along the track, which is, in fact, the old road through the glen, to where it joins the old military road for the final walk to the Kingshouse Hotel some six miles away.

The THIRD SUGGESTED WALK is much shorter and easier. It takes you to Signal Rock, so-called because it is supposed to have been the spot from which the signal was given for the massacre in 1692, though local people feel that this is improbable. The Signal Rock does give a good view of the Glen both east and west. Starting at the Information Centre, you can reach Signal Rock from a footbridge over the Coe about a third of a mile along the A82(T), travelling west towards Glencoe village. The rock tops a knoll near a lochan and the site of one of the Glen's old settlements. The walk and the rock are both pleasantly wooded. You can return to the Information Centre via the minor road which runs behind and to the north of Signal Rock. Along this road to the west is the Leacantuim Youth Hostel, and to the east is the Cachaig Hotel.

20. STEWART OF APPIN AND TICONDEROGA
Barcaldine Castle, near Benderloch

Benderloch is the stretch of land between Loch Creran and Loch Etive in Argyll. It is a strangely shaped area in which an imaginative person might see a similarity to the head of a reindeer with stunted horns looking towards the Firth of Lorn. The part east of the A828 (the head of the reindeer) is steeply hilly, rising to 1000 feet at Beinn Lora which overlooks Ardmuckish Bay to the north of the mouth of Loch Etive. Across the hills, the Forestry Commission's Barcaldine Forest provides a patch of dark green on the otherwise bare hills. West of the A828, the land is flatter (the horns of the reindeer) and extends into the Lynn of Lorn in a broken anvil-shaped peninsula which lies parallel to the island of Lismore and to Appin.

On the Loch Creran side lies Barcaldine Castle, built in the sixteenth century by Duncan Campbell of Glenorchy. This small, typically Scottish 'tower' castle lay in ruins for many years but has now been restored and is open to the public by arrangement at Easter and from July to October. (Telephone Mr Campbell Godley, Ledaig 214).

This pretty castle was the setting of the first act of a bloody drama that, according to legend, had its culmination in front of Fort Ticonderoga in the North American colonies.

It was in the grounds of Barcaldine Castle that, not for the first time, a Campbell fought a Stewart of Appin. With their dirks slashing and plunging at each other the two men fought a long and desperate battle until Donald Campbell fell and was despatched by Stewart.

Realizing that he was now in danger of vengeance from the Campbell kinsmen, Stewart of Appin thought up a

Inverawe House.

cunning and daring idea. He would ride to Inverawe, the Campbell stronghold near Loch Etive before the news of his victim's death reached there and he would ask for hospitality which, by the unwritten law of the Highlands, Duncan Campbell of Inverawe would give him as well as protection from attack.

When he arrived at Inverawe House, Duncan Campbell, brother of the dead man, himself opened the door and welcomed him in, not knowing that his brother Donald lay dead in a stream at Barcaldine.

The evening passed in general conversation, Campbell supplying his guest with food and drink. Having eaten, Stewart of Appin was shown to his room, and Duncan Campbell retired to his, lighting his way by candlelight.

During the night, Duncan Campbell woke with a start to see a pale figure standing by his bed. Rubbing the sleep from his eyes and looking more closely, he saw with a shock of horror that it was his own brother, covered in blood, who stood there.

'What is it, man?' he asked in alarm.

The ghost of Donald Campbell raised an arm and pointed in the direction of the room in which Stewart of Appin slept.

'Brother, you have a Stewart in the house,' the apparition murmured, 'and he is my murderer.'

At this, the phantom disappeared, leaving Duncan Campbell wondering if the visitation had been a dream. And if it was not, what should he do? Highland law forbade him to harm his guest, but perhaps he *was* the murderer of his own brother!

Duncan Campbell fell into a troubled sleep, but once again was awoken by the same apparition who looked at him accusingly.

Though he wished for revenge, the sacred law of hospitality prevented Duncan Campbell from taking his dirk and despatching his guest as he slept, so he decided to let the matter rest till morning and closed his eyes again. But not for long. The ghost was at his bedside again and this time Duncan Campbell tried to explain the reason for his reluctance to revenge his brother then and there.

He saw the expression of scorn and contempt that came upon his brother's waxen face and which none of his explanations would wipe away.

'Brother,' the ghost of Donald Campbell cried as he turned away, 'I will not bother you again until we meet at Ticonderoga.'

Duncan Campbell slept no more that night wondering what the strange appointment might signify and what he would do about Stewart of Appin the following day. About the latter he did not need to concern himself further, for Stewart of Appin was gone by daylight.

Soon after this eerie encounter, Duncan Campbell joined the Black Watch and eventually he found himself with his regiment in America where, at a skirmish with the French for possession of Fort Ticonderoga, his brother's last words came into his mind as an enemy bullet brought his life to an end.

According to local legend, Duncan Campbell returned to his home in ghostly form and may be seen on a moonlight night wandering round the house where his sense of Highland honour betrayed his duty to his own kin.

Barcaldine Castle.

Barcaldine Castle can be reached by a minor road, sign-posted 'South Shian', which turns left (if you are coming from Oban) off the A828(T) at Benderloch. The nearest railway station is Connel on the Glasgow–Oban line, from there is a bus service to Benderloch.

The FIRST SUGGESTED WALK in this area starts at the cross-roads you will come to some one-and-three-quarter miles after you turn off the A828(T). There is sufficient room here to leave a car. At the cross-roads, the narrow road going right gives you a short walk of a hundred yards or so to Barcaldine Castle before continuing on to join up with the A828(T). As we said earlier, you can visit the Castle by arrangement, but you can get a very reasonable view of it from the road.

Back at the cross-roads, take the road ahead, sign-posted 'South Shian'. This short, one-and-a-quarter-mile walk gives you some fine views of Loch Creran. There is a caravan park and a stony beach. At Seabank you will see an oyster hatchery offshore. The road ends at South Shian House, and from this end of the beach you can look back and see the roof of Barcaldine Castle among the trees.

The SECOND SUGGESTED WALK in this area is the Beinn Lora Walk, or Walks, laid out by the Forestry Commission in their Barcaldine Forest. The car park and walks map for this site are at a sign-posted right-hand (if you are coming from Oban) turning off the A828(T) just south of the Benderloch Post Office. You may choose your own walk from suggested routes of one to three miles in length. The walks take you uphill through the forests to the open hill tops, where you will find some magnificent views down the Firth of Lorn.

21. THE RED BOOK OF APPIN
Loch Awe and Loch Etive

Loch Awe is a freshwater loch, though it stretches almost to the Sound of Jura. Its sea exit was blocked at the end of the last Ice Age and when that occurred the waters of Loch Awe had to find their way out to the sea via Loch Etive to the north. This accident of nature created one of the most beautiful inland lochs of Scotland, its twenty-three-mile length vying with Loch Lomond for its variety of scenery. On the west side is the forest of Inverliever, a coniferous forest, which remains green throughout the year but also obscures the views, while the woodland on the east side is deciduous and provides the pageantry of seasonal change. From Cladich to Dalmally at the head of the loch the views, including Ben Cruachan and Kilchurn Castle, are superb.

It was along this part of the lake that there once lived a miller's apprentice, who had the alarming experience of coming face to face with the devil. As is his custom, Satan did not immediately reveal himself but instead appeared as a sympathetic and kindly stranger eager to be of service to an overworked and underpaid young miller. After listening to the young man's tales of woe the devil expressed his concern at the way in which the apprentice was being misused by his master and offered to look into ways in which he could help him. He said that he needed a little time in which to think the matter over and suggested another meeting further away from the miller's neighbourhood. Beinn Mheadhonach on neighbouring Loch Etive, he thought, would be an admirable place on which to meet.

As the miller's lad was a frank and open person by nature

– otherwise he would hardly have talked so freely to a stranger – he told the miller about his meeting with the stranger, warning him that if the stranger's offer was any good he would be leaving the miller's employ. The miller was not as bad a boss as the youth had painted him and he felt a little uneasy on the boy's behalf, so he discussed the matter with the minister of his church. The minister, who knew a thing or two about these benign strangers who would appear from nowhere to offer panaceas for the burdens of this world, thought about it at length. Not wishing to alarm either his friend the miller or the miller's apprentice, he suggested only that if the apprentice were determined to go through with this odd meeting on the slopes of Mheadhonach he ought to at least carry a branch of rowan with him. If he felt at any time that he needed protection, he could then draw a circle on the ground with the rowan and jump inside it.

The miller thought this was strange advice, but he trusted the minister and so prevailed on the boy to do as he suggested. The young lad laughed but agreed to follow the minister's advice and found himself a rowan tree from which he cut a good thick branch. When he arrived on the slopes of the mountain he was still not convinced about the efficacy of the protection he had been advised to carry, but he was certainly glad to have a stout stick with him for it was a dark and stormy night and he felt very much afraid. However, he was too proud to turn back, and carried on steadily to the place on the mountain where he was to meet the stranger.

In the light of the moon that shone fitfully between the racing clouds, the miller's apprentice saw the stranger and he was more than a little relieved not to be alone on the mountain any more. The stranger greeted him and then thrust a red book at him, telling him that before they could begin negotiations he needed to have his signature in the book. The boy opened the book and saw that it was full of writing but in the darkness he was unable to read what it said. Nevertheless, he signed on the page that the stranger indicated to him. Then, some sixth sense warned him of danger. With sudden misgiving he closed the book and put it under his arm, at the same time grasping the rowan staff firmly with his right hand and drawing a line between himself and the stranger just as the latter was stepping forward to take the book.

The stranger ran along the line but the boy was too quick for him, sweeping the rowan staff around him in a circle as he had been told to do. As the circle was completed, the stranger seemed suddenly to explode in a searing flash of light which momentarily blinded the young man. When he opened his eyes to look again at the stranger he saw not the kindly old man who had promised to improve his situation but the malevolent and furious face of the devil. The young man felt that his last moment had come but as the devil did not reach out for him as he expected he knew that the protection provided by the rowan circle was real. Still frightened but a little reassured, the boy kept the book that the devil was demanding of him firmly under his arm.

Now the devil began a war of nerves to confuse the young apprentice and drive him out of his circle. First he turned himself into a greyhound and ran dizzily round and round the circle, then he transformed himself into a bull and snorted and pawed at the edges of the circle, terrifying the young man inside it. When that failed to dislodge him, the devil became a flock of crows that dived over and over again above the youth's head. While all these and similar onslaughts were taking place, the young apprentice did his best to keep his head and, standing firm in the centre of the circle, thought of the miller whose generous nature had given him the only protection he now had.

All night long the devil tried every trick he could think of to force the boy to leave his safe circle but he failed and as dawn broke he gave a great howl of frustration and shot off

Pass of Brander, Loch Awe.

into the clouds, leaving a trail of sulphurous steam in his wake.

What happened to the Red Book of Appin, the legend does not tell us. Sufficient to say, the miller's apprentice had learnt his lesson and knew to beware in future of strangers bearing great promises.

THE WALK:
FROM ARDCHATTAN
PRIORY TO BONAWE
QUARRIES, RETURNING
TO ARDCHATTAN.

MAP SQUARE:
Ordnance Survey Sheet
49/981351
A very pretty lochside walk, 3 miles for the round trip, skirting the south-west foot of Beinn Mheadhonach.

Of the two areas in which this story is set – Loch Awe and Beinn Mheadhonach on Loch Etive – we have chosen the latter near which to site a walk. This delightful lochside walk starts at Ardchattan Priory on the northern shore of lower Loch

Etive. From Oban, seven miles away, the Priory is reached via the A828(T): cross Connel Bridge then turn right on to the un-numbered minor road along the loch.

Ardchattan Priory is a suitable place from which to begin a walk in search of the devil and his Red Book, for it was a religious house for several centuries, and has the additional cachet of having suffered at the hands of Cromwell's soldiers, being burnt in 1654. The remains of the Priory may be visited at any time, but are particularly pleasant to see from April to September, when the gardens of adjoining Ardchattan House are open to the public.

From Ardchattan, where there is parking space for a few cars, follow the road east along the lochside and then inland for half a mile to the junction with the B845. Here, the slopes of Beinn Mheadhonach rise above the loch and the road. From here east to Bonawe Quarries, a distance of a mile, the road becomes very attractive, constantly switchbacking up and down hillocks and rises in the road, through trees and woodland along the loch's edge. The switchback nature of the road means that this short walk is quite strenuous, for the rises and falls, though small, are quite steep.

The road proper ends at Bonawe Quarries, beside a rather derelict collection of offices, abandoned workers' dwellings and equipment which nevertheless offer a suggestion of the busier days of the quarries' heyday. They are still worked, of course, and the quarry office at the gates is usually manned on working days, where you may make your presence known if you wish to walk through the quarries to reach the path beyond to the upper arm of Loch Etive. There is usually no objection to your doing so.

Our SUGGESTED WALK ends at the quarries, however, and you may return to Ardchattan by the same route, making a round trip of some three miles, or you may catch the Oban bus in Bonawe village.

22. DEIRDRE OF THE SORROWS
Loch Etive

The L-shaped sea loch that enters the Firth of Lorn at Connel barely escapes being an inland loch for across its mouth there lies a submerged barrier of rocks that, had it been a few feet higher, would have made a bridge between Benderloch and Lorn. From the iron railway bridge (now used for road transport) that crosses the loch the rocks can be clearly seen and as the tide recedes they emerge above the water's surface creating a series of rapids called the Falls of Lora.

On the seaward side, the waters of the loch run past the islands of Eilean Mor and Eilean Beag, fragments of land which are really a continuation of the peninsula on which Dunstaffnage Castle stands (see p. 152). To the north, in Benderloch, is the flat promontory on which Connel airport provides a landing strip for Logan Air flights to and from Glasgow and Mull.

The lower arm of the loch has a pleasantly green and pastoral look, with hills rising away to each side. Along the lakeside, Highland cattle graze contentedly in the fields, and herons, cormorants and other sea birds are a common sight. Here and there on the promontories jutting out into the waters of the loch, fine grey stone houses have been built, surrounded by splendid gardens. At Auchnacloich House the gardens are open in spring by courtesy of the owner and are well worth a visit for they are a splendid sight with the spring flowers flooding the lawns and great azalea bushes standing brilliant with colour against a background of trees that include the remains of the oldest oak forest in Britain.

Loch Etive.

A little further along the lake, with Ben Cruachan in full view on a clear day and the more sombre rocky valley of the upper loch funnelling the view up towards Rannoch Moor, lies the village of Taynuilt. Here was once a well-known iron foundry which made cannons for Nelson and where Bonawe furnace, which was fuelled by oak from the once-extensive forest, is a well-preserved feature of industrial archaeology. There is a pier at Taynuilt from which, in summer, boats leave for excursions up the loch and from where there are fine views of the legendary home of Deirdre of the Sorrows. Though the exact site of her home is not known, this whole area of the loch is closely associated with her poignant story.

Deirdre was the daughter of a Pictish king whose kingdom extended over northern Ireland and Loch Etive. She spent her youth near Auchnacloich and the loch shores between that village and Taynuilt provided the playground for Deirdre and her friends, the three sons of Uisneach, boys about her age who had grown up with her and had shared all the pleasures of life along the lochside.

The foursome were almost like one family and young enough to enjoy each others' company in an unselfconscious but intimate way. At the height of this idyllic moment in their lives, the friends received a stunning blow. Deirdre, they were told abruptly, was to leave for Ireland to live at the court of King Conchobar of Ulster to whom her father had promised her. Had it not been for her friendship with the sons of Uisneach, the girl might have gone obediently, for at that time it was not unusual for fathers to give away their daughters in return for a treaty of alliance or some other worldly gain. But Deirdre's love for her companions gave her courage to defy her father and King Conchobar, and she refused to go to Ireland. She would, she vowed, rather die than leave the sons of Uisneach.

Her determined manner greatly concerned the men sent by King Conchobar to escort Deirdre to Ireland. They conferred with her family to decide how they could best persuade her to board the ship that had been sent for her.

After some discussion, a compromise was reached by which the sons of Uisneach would be allowed to accompany Deirdre to Ireland if she would honour her father's promise to Conchobar and agree to marry the Celtic king.

Realizing that a total refusal to leave Loch Etive would not be accepted Deirdre acquiesced, though she did not look forward to her journey and even less to her formal betrothal to the king she had never seen. It was during her voyage across the sea to Ireland that she expressed her misgivings and her sadness at leaving the land of her childhood in the series of songs associated with her name, and made famous by the bard Ossian.

Once she had reached King Conchobar's castle, Deirdre felt no less unhappy and as the months passed and the preparations for her wedding began, her distress became obvious to all those about her. Even King Conchobar, usually a busy man concerned with his own affairs, noticed Deirdre's listless air and this angered him for he had planned a splendid wedding in keeping with his position and it hardly flattered him to find that his bride was so clearly lacking in joy at the forthcoming event.

Being a practical man, Conchobar sought a quick remedy for his problem and it did not take him long to reason that the obstacle to his happy marriage was his betrothed's relationship with the three young men who had accompanied her to Ireland. The answer was to get rid of them, which Conchobar did in the barbaric manner of his times. He had them killed.

This ruthless deed, as was hardly surprising, had the very opposite effect to what Conchobar had hoped. Deirdre became more withdrawn than ever, speaking to no one and staring endlessly out of the castle windows, her thoughts obviously far away. Though Conchobar pressed on with the preparations for the wedding, he had forebodings of disaster and it hardly came as a surprise to him when Dierdre began to pine away.

As she lay dying, Deirdre expressed the wish that she might be buried with her childhood friends and the pathos of her situation touched the hearts even of the tough men at Conchobar's court. The grave of the sons of Uisneach was opened and the dead Deirdre was laid beside them.

(A quite different version of the story has Deirdre fleeing with the sons of Uisneach from the wrath of King Conchobar and making her way back to lonely Glen Etive where she lived thereafter.)

THE WALKS:	MAP SQUARE:
1. FROM THE A85 WEST OF TAYNUILT TO AIRDS BAY.	1. Ordnance Survey Sheet 49/996315
2. A FOREST TRACK WALK NEAR INVERAWE HOUSE.	2. Ordnance Survey Sheet 50/022316 An easy walk along a quiet road and the loch shore; and a more adventurous one on forest tracks, which may be muddy, so stout shoes are needed.

By car, Loch Etive can be reached from Oban or Perth on the A85(T), and from Fort William on the A828. The most interesting walks on the Deirdre of the Sorrows (south) side of the loch start from the A85(T).

For A SHORT WALK to the wooded shore where Deirdre spent many childhood hours, drive or walk west out of Taynuilt on the A85(T) for about a mile, and look for a signpost indicating Airds Bay off to the right. This is a minor road starting between two stone pillars, and leads to a small house where there is a gate across the road. Go through the gate (make sure you close it behind you, as livestock graze here) and carry on down to the loch shore. If you have come by car this far, rather than walking from Taynuilt, you can leave your vehicle anywhere along this stretch and then walk along the grassy shore. The distance is barely a mile from the main road – or two miles if you have walked from Taynuilt – to where the road ends at two private houses, but it makes a pleasant walk. The grassy lochside makes a delightful spot for a picnic.

For A LONGER WALK in this area, drive out of Taynuilt east along the A85(T) towards the Pass of Brander for about two and a half miles. Turn off at Bridge of Awe on to the Inverawe road sign-posted on your left. This minor road is very pretty, with many silver birch trees and several streams and lochans (small ponds), and runs in a northerly direction to the loch. When you reach a fork, take the right-hand road; the left-hand route leads down to the private Inverawe House, which you may have seen from the A85(T). There is a path over a suspension bridge to the house, which was the place from which Campbell of Argyll set out to attack the 'bonnie house of Airlie', as well as being the scene of Duncan Campbell's vision of Ticonderoga (see p. 129).

As you approach the rear of Inverawe House, you will see a forest road going uphill to the right. This is the beginning of your walk through the forest. Park your car at the Inverawe House car park and walk back about a third of a mile to the track, which is marked 'Port na Mine'. This goes through a coniferous forest planted by the Forestry Commission, and after a mile you will find yourself at the lochside. After three miles, you arrive at the River Noe and the end of the track, so you must retrace your path.

An alternative route on this walk is to follow the track leading directly from the car park to the loch – about a mile. You can then walk along a path that skirts the lochside and joins up with the forest path.

23. BLACK COLIN AND HIS FAITHFUL WIFE
Kilchurn Castle

The awesome ruins of Kilchurn Castle stand in marshy ground on a peninsula at the top of beautiful Loch Awe where the Orchy and the Strae flow into the loch, and near Loch Awe village. Behind the castle a mass of hill upon hill and mountain ranges culminating in Ben Cruachan rise into the sky. It is a splendid and beautiful scene.

The guidebooks say that the castle was begun in 1440 by Sir Colin Campbell of Glenorchy, who had married an heiress, Margaret Stewart. This Colin Campbell, called *Cailean Mor* – Black Colin – of Loch Awe, was the second son of the Duncan Campbell who was ancestor of the Earls and Dukes of Argyll. Duncan gave his son Glenorchy Castle which stood on an islet, Innis Eilean, at the head of Loch Awe, and here Colin founded the Campbell of Breadalbane clan. He is known to have visited Rome at

Kilchurn Castle, Loch Awe.

least three times and fought with the Knights of St John against the Moslems, hence his nickname 'The Black Knight of Rhodes'.

Legend, interwoven with known historical facts, provides a far more romantic account of the origins of Kilchurn Castle than do the guide books.

Black Colin of Loch Awe, young, impetuous and longing for adventure, even if it would have taken him from the side of his beautiful wife whom he loved dearly, was so inspired by tales of the Crusades told him by a wandering bard who came to Glenorchy Castle, that he determined to join them himself and fight the Infidel in the far-off lands of the Eastern Mediterranean.

His preparations were long and difficult, for he knew he would be away for several years. It might even be that he would be killed fighting for Christendom, or die on the terrible journey. Before he left, therefore, he gave his wife one half of a ring which he had had made specially for the purpose, and which carried both their names in the design. The other half he kept, telling his wife that should he ever come to his death bed he would, as he lay dying, give his half of the ring to a trusted servant to be brought back to her, so that she would know her husband was indeed dead.

For seven years, Margaret Campbell waited for her husband, whom she loved as strongly as he loved her, to come back to Scotland. At the end of that time, her position became difficult and dangerous. The Campbell lands were surrounded by lands of the MacGregors, MacIntyres and MacCorquodales, any of whom might try to take for themselves lands with no lord to protect them.

Then Neil MacCorquodale came wooing Margaret Campbell. He pointed out to her that, under Scottish law, she was free to marry again now that her husband had been absent for seven years and no word had come from him. She hesitated and prevaricated. Her husband would have contrived to send her a token as notice of his death, but none had come. What token? asked MacCorquodale, but she would not say.

MacCorquodale grew cunning. He forged a letter from Black Colin which, he told Margaret, would have had the token with it but that the servant bringing it had been robbed of all his possessions including the token on his journey from Rome.

So it seemed as if Black Colin were dead, and Margaret could hesitate no longer. She agreed to marry Neil MacCorquodale, but said she must first build a castle to her husband's memory. Employing a ruse similar to that used by Penelope when waiting for the return of Ulysses, Margaret ordered her workmen to build as slowly as possible.

Thus Kilchurn Castle began slowly to rise on the shores of Loch Awe. Eventually it was finished, and the day came when Margaret Campbell must marry Neil MacCorquodale.

But there was one other woman in Glenorchy who loved Black Colin well and who did not believe that he was dead. This was his old foster mother, who sent her own son off to Rome to try to discover the truth. He reached Rome safely and found Black Colin there alive and well. Colin had had many adventures since leaving Scotland and was amazed, and perhaps a little guilty, when he realized how long he had been away. He was also greatly distressed to hear of his wife's troubles, and set off for Scotland with all speed.

Black Colin arrived in Glenorchy on the wedding day. He went to the pre-nuptial feast, to which all people in the region were invited, in disguise so that if he thought that his wife was happy in her coming marriage, then he would disappear quietly again unobserved. He soon found an opportunity to slip his half of the ring into her hand, looking into her face as he did so, so that she might know who he was but know also that she could consider him dead if she so wished. Of course Margaret greeted her husband with joy and gladness, Neil MacCorquodale retired discomforted, and the happy pair lived long and lovingly together in the new castle which the faithful wife had built.

Kilchurn Castle prospered for some centuries, being enlarged several times, and the Campbells of Breadalbane lived in it until 1740. It was occupied by government troops after the rising of '45, and fell into disrepair during the nineteenth century, partly because its roofing materials were thriftily removed for use in another Campbell of Breadalbane castle and partly because severe storms also took their toll of the fabric. The great storm of 1879, which wrecked the Tay Bridge, also blew a great chunk off one of Kilchurn's corner towers.

THE WALK:	MAP SQUARE:
A SHORT, COMFORTABLE WALK ROUND KILCHURN CASTLE.	Ordnance Survey Sheet 50/143276 An easy walk allowing the visitor to see Kilchurn Castle close at hand. Watch out for marshy ground!

Kilchurn Castle lies off the A85(T) twenty-one miles from Oban. The road comes down the Pass of Brander, a narrow valley with steep, rocky slopes through which the water of Loch Awe flows into Loch Etive. Brander was the scene of a famous encounter between Robert the Bruce and the Macdonalds. To the north of the Pass rises the splendid bulk of Ben Cruachan (3689 feet). The Cruachan Hydro-Electric Power Station built in a huge cavern inside Ben Cruachan, said to be one of the biggest quarrying operations ever completed in Britain, can be visited Mondays to Fridays from Easter to October, while from June to August it is also open at weekends.

To the east of Loch Awe lies the attractive Glen Orchy. Loch Awe itself is also very beautiful, with a drive along its eastern shore being particularly memorable. The road here is the A819, which branches off the A85(T) just past Kilchurn Castle to wind its way to the southern end of the loch through attractively wooded scenery and past several hamlets. From the A819, at its northern end, is a fine view of Kilchurn Castle. There are two notable castles on inlets in Loch Awe also worth viewing from the A819. First, at the entrance to the Brander arm of the loch is Fraoch Eilean. The other, further south, is InchConnell.

The walk here is a pleasant and easy one along the flat peninsula on which Kilchurn Castle stands, though walkers should check the state of the ground before setting off as it can be very marshy. Start at the gate on the loch side of the straight stretch of the A819 near the top of the loch. You walk across a gated railway line to reach the castle grounds. The castle is not open to the public as it is undergoing restoration, but it can be viewed close-up from the outside. You will see a great central tower, built by Black Colin, surrounded by walls and four tall corner turrets, which were built in the sixteenth century. There is also a courtyard, whose buildings indicate a once-fine mansion.

24. THE MURDERED BRIDEGROOM
Dunstaffnage Castle, near Oban

Although Dunstaffnage Bay has been built round with housing estates, the castle itself stands isolated on its peninsula in the midst of a small green park. It is obvious at a glance that this was an easily defended position surrounded by sea and approachable only though a narrow peninsula. The castle once controlled the shipping routes in and out of Loch Etive and its bay is still a popular anchorage for cruising along the coast.

There has been a castle on this site since at least the thirteenth century, and its history has been eventful. It was attacked by Robert the Bruce, taken by Cromwell, and burned in 1685. Flora MacDonald was imprisoned in it for a short while in 1746 for helping Bonnie Prince Charlie to escape. It was destroyed by fire in the early part of the nineteenth century but has recently been restored.

Today, it is an imposing sight with its solid grey walls and towers standing amid green woods and grassy slopes, and like many other Scottish castles evokes the hazardous times of medieval Scotland. In its grounds is a ruined, centuries-old chapel, where an extraordinary drama once took place. This was the wedding of the Lord of Lorn, John Stewart.

Dunstaffnage Castle originally belonged to the MacDougalls and had passed to the Stewarts by marriage, though the MacDougalls had never given up hope of owning it once more. Their opportunity came early in the fifteenth century. Sir James Stewart, who was an old man, had no legal heir but his daughters had all married into the Campbell clan. The husband of one of them was the ambitious and ruthless Colin Campbell, Earl of Argyll,

150

who now waited for the old man to die in order to seize his castle and lands.

Sir James was old, but not feeble, and he was determined that his lands would not fall into Campbell hands. He did have one, illegitimate, son and in order to keep out the Campbells, he decided to legalize the position of his bastard son by marrying the boy's mother. He sent a messenger to her telling her to come to Dunstaffnage with her son Dugald so that the ceremony could take place.

The plans for the wedding got under way and all the friends and kinsmen of Sir James were invited, including the Campbells who, as relatives, could hardly be excluded. They were already plotting to ensure that the marriage would not take place.

On the day of the planned wedding the guests gathered in the chapel while the bridegroom and his bride prepared themselves in the castle. Sir James and his bride-to-be walked from the castle over the grass to the chapel where the priest who was to perform the ceremony awaited them. The Campbells and other close kinsmen were gathered there, too.

As Sir James arrived at the chapel door Alan MacDougall, who had been chosen to perform the foul deed, ran forward, drew his dagger and plunged it into the bridegroom's side. There was a cry of horror from the assembled company and then confusion as everyone pressed forward to aid the dying Earl. Taking advantage of the turmoil, Alan MacDougall made his getaway while his Campbell kinsmen protested their horror at the deed.

While some people shouted for their horses to set after MacDougall and others cried out for a doctor, the priest, maintaining his composure, whispered to Sir James that he would carry out the wedding ceremony and thus confound the Campbell plot.

With his dying breath, Sir James whispered the words of the marriage ceremony and placed his family ring on the bride's finger, while his son Dugald, now the legitimate heir to the castle and its lands, looked on grimly.

Not long after this horrific day, Dugald revenged his father's death by defeating the MacDougalls in battle at Bridge of Orchy.

THE WALK:	MAP SQUARE:
FROM OBAN TO DUN-STAFFNAGE CASTLE, VIA DUNOLLIE CASTLE AND GANAVAN.	Ordnance Survey Sheet 49/859302 A 4-mile walk along the coast.

Dunstaffnage lies off the A85 between Oban and Connel, both of which places are served by the railway line between Glasgow and Oban. Several bus routes lie along this road.

Because it sits on a small peninsula, the castle itself cannot provide any lengthy walks in its vicinity, apart from the immediate grounds, which are well cared for, with good places for picnics overlooking the sea and the tiny fishing-boat jetty.

By the A85, Dunstaffnage is three miles from Oban, but if

Dunstaffnage Castle.

you take the minor, coast road out of Oban, the route is nearer four miles long, and very pleasant.

Starting point for this walk is on the Corran Esplanade in Oban. This route passes some of the town's main hotels and the two cathedrals as it skirts the waterfront, so the views are interesting on both sides. After a little less than three-quarters of a mile, you will pass the lighthouse at Port Mor and then, after a few hundred yards, Dunollie Castle, standing high on a bluff above the road.

This historic castle, once the principal seat of the MacDougalls, Lords of Lorn, is a ruin whose walls are dangerous, so it cannot be entered, but you can walk round its perimeter. Look out on the right for the Dog Stone, a tall pillar of rock which legend has it was the post to which Fingal tied his hunting dog, Bran.

Past Dunollie, you are now skirting Camas Ban ('White Bay'). There are some caves on your right.

Just over a mile from Dunollie, the road ends at Ganavan where there is a putting green, beach, caravan site and tearooms, though a track goes on towards Dunollie Beg and the A85. You should keep straight on, leaving the road for the path you will find at the northern end of the beach car park. This path goes north on to the edge of the golf course, turns right at the club house, and cuts across this hillocky heathland to the A85. (It is better to follow the path to the A85, even though it means you must follow the main road for a stretch, as the unpathed land due north to Dunstaffnage is farmland and inclined to be marshy.)

Follow the A85 for just under half a mile, until you come to a track going left just south of the camping and caravan site. This track skirts the western edge of Dunbeg village, an uninspiring modern development, and comes out at the bottom of the Dunstaffnage peninsula by Dunstaffnage Farm.

The remaining walk to the castle, past the Dunstaffnage Marine Research Laboratory, is just a quarter of a mile. You will find a well-preserved thirteenth-century castle with

153

round towers and a curtain wall. In the grounds are the remains of the castle's small chapel. Opening hours for the castle are: April–September, 09.30–19.00, weekdays and 14.00–19.00 Sundays; October–March, 09.30–16.00 weekdays, and 14.00–16.00 Sundays.

25. THE THREE-SCORE FOOLS OF LORN
Craignish

The western coast of Nether Lorn which lies just south of the Isle of Mull is full of islands and small lochs, among which are Loch Melfort and Loch Craignish. Melfort lies to the north a few miles from Oban and although it is a sea loch, appears almost landlocked because of the islands – Luing, Shuna and Scarba – that protect its entrance. To the south of the loch rises Tom Soilleir (1199 feet) and one of the mountain's spurs extends into the sea as a promontory. Arduaine House is situated here; once a seat of the Campbells, it is now a hotel. Arduaine Gardens, behind the hotel, are open to the public.

Over a pass to the south lies Loch Craignish, also a sea loch which, seen from the vantage point of the A816(T) up the Pass of Bealach Mor to the south, looks to be full of islands. The land slopes down to the sea at the ends of the loch and on the northern peninsula is Craignish Castle which also was once a Campbell possession. It is now a private mansion though the gardens are open to the public in May and June; they are particularly interesting for the rhododendron plantings were laid out by the same Osgood Mackenzie who created the famous Inverewe Gardens near Poolewe.

This dramatic area of rugged coastlines and islands among which the racing tide has wrecked many ships, is the scene of a legend whose black humour is appropriate to the fratricidal encounters of Highland clans.

The story starts with a MacDougall of Lorn who had ten sons to each of whom he gave a piece of land in Lorn. One of the sons was called Callum Colgainn and in due course he, too, became the father of a great many sons, twelve to be exact.

One day, when Callum and all his sons were attending church, a strange dark-haired woman stopped old MacDougall and asked him who the handsome family of young men were. Dougall told her that they were his grandchildren, the sons of Callum Colgainn. The old lady looked them over carefully, then gripped MacDougall's arm and told him that one of the young men would one day have a third of Scotland all to himself.

MacDougall felt distinctly uneasy at the possible implications of this cryptic prophecy but as time went by and nothing occurred to alter the even tenor of the lives of his family he forgot the incident. Then, one day, something happened which brought the prophecy back to him. One of the sons of Callum Colgainn died mysteriously of a disease which no one could identify. Then another died, and another, until only two sons of Callum were left.

Concerned for their welfare, grandfather MacDougall encouraged them to leave home and settle far away from each other so that the dreadful curse that had fallen on the family would have less chance of falling on both of them together.

The two surviving sons of Callum Colgainn loaded their belongings on to their horses and rode off in opposite directions. In due course, each settled in a new home, one in the north in Glen Etive and the other in the south in Knapdale. Their lives were uneventful and happy for many years. Each of them had children who in turn had their own children until each of their families numbered thirty people.

Each family, now called MacCallum, received occasional news of the other family and, as they grew older, the brothers, now chiefs of their own families, still retained a yearning to see each other. Finally, they decided that since nothing unpleasant had happened to them in the years since they had left home, it would be safe for them to meet again. MacCallum of Knapdale therefore sent a message to his brother MacCallum of Loch Etive inviting him to bring his whole family over for a visit. By coincidence, MacCallum of Loch Etive had written to his brother at the same time.

Each of them, not waiting for a reply from the other, set off to see his brother expecting to surprise him as he waited for the reply to his message.

The two groups of people travelled along the road that runs by the sea past Craignish Loch and Loch Melfort and at a point more or less halfway between the two lochs they came face to face at a narrow ford crossing. The brothers had not seen each other for many years and were no longer the young men whose images remained in their imaginations, so it is not surprising that they did not recognize each other. All that each one saw was a band of people blocking the way ahead and, being impatient to get on with their journey, each shouted at the other to stand aside in order to allow the passage of their own party.

Tempers became heated as each refused to allow the other's party to cross the ford first until finally the younger and more impetuous hot-blooded members of the two groups drew their claymores and began to fight in the shallow waters of the ford. At first, some of the more even-tempered members of both sides called on the combatants to stop, but as soon as blood began to flow their desire for revenge overcame their common-sense and very quickly every one was involved in the affray.

The battle was hard and no quarter was given until finally only one man from each side was left standing alive among the corpses whose blood stained the waters of the river. These two, one an older man from Glen Etive and the other a youth from Knapdale, looked at each other with their claymores raised and hatred in their hearts and eyes.

They were exhausted by the battle and so they did not move immediately. Slowly the realization came to each of them that they were the last living member of their family, though each did not know that this was true of the other.

The older man from Glen Etive shook his head sadly and told the younger man that this was a sad day for the MacCallum family who had been on the way from Glen Etive to see their kinsmen at Knapdale. On hearing this, the young man dropped his weapon and replied that he too was a MacCallum and that he and his party had been on the way from Knapdale to Glen Etive to meet his father's kinsfolk. The men stared at each other, horror and disbelief on their faces, until finally the older man staggered towards the younger baring his breast and calling on him to finish his work for he no longer had any wish to live. The younger man turned away, overcome by the horrible events of the day. As he walked back to the river bank he heard a cry and turning round, found the old man on his knees with his own dagger impaled in his chest. The young man from Knapdale was now alone, the sole survivor of the MacCallums and, if not the ruler of a third of Scotland, at least the owner of all the MacCallum lands. Thus was fulfilled the prophecy made to old MacDougall on the church steps so many years before.

THE WALKS:
1. ALONG LOCH CRAIG-
   NISH TO CRAIGNISH
   CASTLE.
2. A HILL WALK UP THE
   PASS OF MELFORT.

MAP SQUARE:
Ordnance Survey Sheet
   55/805044

2. Ordnance Survey Sheet
   55/838843
Two walks, chosen to give a walk north and south of the country in which the legend of the three-score fools is set.

The country between the two sea lochs, Melfort and Craignish, is hilly and bracken-covered, and the island-dotted shore has several safe yacht anchorages, including the Kilmelford Yacht Haven near Arduaine. Kilmelford, a small fishing village, is the largest community in the area.

Craignish lies twenty-six miles south of Oban, on the A816(T) facing the Isle of Jura. It can also be reached by car from Loch Awe on the A840, which joins the A816(T) south of Craignish and from the south via Loch Fyne on the A83, which branches off the Glasgow road at Tarbet on Loch Lomond.

Apart from the two walks suggested, two other places offer the visitor interesting walks. Arduaine Gardens, which have already been mentioned, lie behind the Lochmelfort Hotel at Arduaine and are open every day from April to October. There is a rock garden, also a water garden, in the grounds, where the rhododendrons, azaleas and magnolias are spectacular. Just over a mile south of Arduaine, at Barrichbeyan, is the Argyll Wildlife Centre, whose visitor facilities include a café, bar and toilets. From the other side of the A816(T), opposite the Wildlife Centre's car park, a track going up into the hills makes a pleasant walk.

The FIRST SUGGESTED WALK is a pleasant one following the shores of Loch Craignish. Start at the village of Ardfern, which is on the B8002, about a mile and a half from the turning off the A816(T) and follow the road to the head of Loch Beag, a distance of about three and a half miles, where Craignish Castle stands on a promontory. The castle keep dates from the sixteenth century, but the rest of the present house is much more modern. Craignish gardens may be visited in May and June. From the point, and from the hill behind, you will get a good view of the islands of Scarba and Jura and the tide race which flows from between them.

The SECOND SUGGESTED WALK begins at the head of Loch Melfort, and is a good hill walk up the old road that climbs the Pass of Melfort. Join it at the bridge to Melfort

House over the Oude River. The track follows the eastern bank of the river up the Pass. Where the river broadens, the track joins the A816(T). Return the same way, or take a longer walk back south along the A816(T), branching off to your right just south of Loch nan Druimnean on to the minor road back to Melfort. The walk up the Pass is about one and a half miles, and the route back via the A816(T) is about two miles.

26. THE CARPENTER MACPHEIGH
Loch Gilp

Loch Gilp is an inlet on the northern side of Loch Fyne just above Knapdale. When the tide is out there is a mile of sand at the upper end of the loch at the head of which is Lochgilphead, a small market town with stone houses, many of which have been painted in pastel colours. The centre of the town is the market square on the lochside, and most of the shops and cafés are here. About two miles south of Lochgilphead along the loch is Ardrishaig, the Loch Gilp end of the Crinan Canal which cuts through Knapdale to the Sound of Jura. During the summer the canal which passes to the west of Lochgilphead presents a busy appearance as yachts and motorboats sail through its fifteen locks.

The Crinan Canal.

It was by the shores of this attractive loch that the legendary carpenter MacPheigh, who outwitted the rival carpenters of Lochlann, is supposed to have had his home.

MacPheigh was said by everyone who knew him, and many who didn't, to be the best carpenter in Scotland, something which MacPheigh himself was not averse to believing. His reputation spread far and wide, and inevitably reached other carpenters in Scotland most of whom thought they were just as good as MacPheigh, though they did not bother to do anything about it. The carpenters of Lochlann, however, were so irritated by this claim that they decided to challenge MacPheigh in order to find out just how good a carpenter he was.

Determined to win the encounter, the Lochlann men began their campaign with a psychological attack by announcing to MacPheigh that they would arrive for the challenge not on foot or on horseback or even in a carriage but mounted on wooden horses made by themselves and able to ride across the sea.

MacPheigh was duly impressed and not being a stupid man, he set about some psychological warfare of his own devising. Putting on the apron of his chief assistant, he told his deputy to don the garments which he himself usually wore and, when the carpenters of Lochlann arrived, to pretend that he was the boss of the workshop.

The assistant did as he was told and when the Lochlann carpenters arrived they found him busy giving orders to MacPheigh as if he had been doing so all his life. Having deceived them into thinking that he was MacPheigh, the deputy greeted them and then told them that as far as he was concerned, their visit gave him so much pleasure that he had decided to give up work for that day. 'However,' he added, 'the rest of my men will carry on and you can judge for yourself how practised they are in their craft. Especially this one here,' he added, pointing out the real MacPheigh. 'Though not as good as I am, he is coming on very well and may one day reach the standards that I have attained.'

While the Lochlann carpenters expressed their disappointment at not being able to watch the master at work, the real MacPheigh set about putting a new handle on an axe. First he called for a block on which to work. One of his fellow carpenters went into the yard and brought back a large misshapen stone which made all the Lochlann carpenters laugh because it seemed a very amateurish way to carry on. MacPheigh was not put out and, feigning indifference to their laughter, he covered the stone with a cloth and began to whittle a piece of wood on it. His knife flashed up and down the wood and in a short while he held up an axe handle so well proportioned and smoothly finished that it looked as if it had been planed and sanded.

When it came to fitting the handle into the head of the axe MacPheigh gazed hard and often at the hole that it would fit into and scraped away a little here and a little there until he was sure the top of the handle would fit perfectly. Not once did he take a measurement other than by his eye and the Lochlann carpenters looked on unbelievingly. Having smoothed the top of the axe handle, MacPheigh set up the axe-head with the socket facing him and with a deft flick of the wrist threw the handle into place. There was a sigh from the assembled carpenters which MacPheigh pretended to ignore, nonchalantly clipping his nails with axe blows the while.

Alarmed at the incredible expertise of a mere assistant, the Lochlann carpenters looked at each other anxiously and, at a nod from their leader, retired to a corner of the workshop for a discussion.

When they returned, MacPheigh was putting up some roof rafters, whittling the pegs that held them together and throwing them into holes where the rafters were to be joined, driving home the pegs by throwing the hammer at them so accurately that only one blow was needed.

The false MacPheigh then waved the real MacPheigh

away, telling him that he had done enough for one day. He then addressed himself to the visitors, saying that now that they had seen what his assistant could do he would be prepared to meet them himself in a contest the following day. MacPheigh, watching them from behind a stack of timber, was pleased to observe that the Lochlann men looked thoroughly discomfited.

After repairing to the local inn to restore their flagging spirits at the thought of the next day's encounter, the Lochlann carpenters told the bogus MacPheigh that since they were visiting Loch Gilp for the first time they did not want to miss the opportunity of exploring the countryside and they intended to do so on their wooden horses.

MacPheigh, who was hiding outside the inn, guessed that the Lochlann carpenters were in fact planning to make a getaway to avoid the following day's competition. He ran quickly to the lochside where the wooden horses were drawn up on the shore and removed from each of them some of the vital pegs that held them together.

The legend does not make it clear whether MacPheigh did so with evil intent or merely to prevent the flight of the Lochlann men. What it does say is that when the Lochlann carpenters on their wooden horses had reached the middle of the loch, a great wind arose and the horses fell to pieces. The Lochlann riders all drowned, leaving MacPheigh without any challengers whatsoever to his title of the greatest carpenter in all Scotland – and England, Wales and Ireland as well, for that matter.

THE WALKS:

1. LOCHGILPHEAD TO ARDRISHAIG, RETURNING ALONG THE A83.
2. LOCHGILPHEAD TO CAIRNBAAN, RETURNING ALONG THE SAME ROUTE.

MAP SQUARE:
Ordnance Survey Sheet 55/857879

These two walks along the Crinan Canal both start at the same point. They are not difficult, and are suitable for children, though youngsters must be watched as the canal is, naturally enough, not fenced.

Lochgilphead lies on the A83 between Ardrishaig and Inveraray, on a small loch running north from Loch Fyne at the frontier between Argyll and Knapdale. There are low hills round the two-mile long Loch Gilp and the A83 skirts the loch as it heads south down the Kintyre peninsula.

Lochgilphead makes a good centre for excursions into Kintyre and Knapdale, though it is not highly developed as a tourist resort. On the eastern shore of Loch Gilp lies Kilmorey Castle, and further up Loch Fyne is Inveraray, a charming and well-maintained town dominated by Inveraray Castle, home of the chief of the Clan Campbell since the fourteenth century, though the present castle was rebuilt in the eighteenth century.

The Crinan Canal, one end of which is at Ardrishaig, two miles south of Lochgilphead, was cut between 1793 and 1801 at the height of Britain's canal-building boom to provide a short, safe passage from Loch Fyne to the Atlantic, avoiding the stormy trip round the Mull of Kintyre. Today, it is used mainly by yachts and holiday cruisers, though fishing boats and other coastal craft may also be seen on it. The canal is nine miles long, has fifteen locks, and its Atlantic end is at Crinan.

It is possible to walk the whole length of the canal, for the towpath is a good one, but the two walks suggested here are shorter. Both begin just out of Lochgilphead at its western side, where the A83 bends round in front of the town. It is advisable to leave your car in the town, as there is not a lot of space for vehicles where the walk begins.

For the FIRST SUGGESTED WALK cross the bridge over the canal, turn left, and walk along the canal's edge south to its starting point at the sea lock near Ardrishaig lighthouse and pier. This part of the walk is about two miles long, and skirts low hills whose burns drain down to the loch, passing a distillery and three sets of locks in Ardrishaig. Return back along the canal or on the A83 which skirts the shores of the loch.

The SECOND SUGGESTED WALK, from the same starting point, is in the opposite direction. The canal's towpath is on the eastern side of the loch, and to the three sets of locks at Cairbaan, a small town with a hotel and restaurant, is about two miles of easy walking through pleasant scenery. Return along the same route.

F

MULL

The Lady Rock
The Duque de Florencia
The Hunchbacks of Iona

27. THE LADY ROCK
Duart Castle

The car ferry and steamer that run from Oban to
Craignure on the Isle of Mull pass between the Isle of
Lismore on their starboard side and a small rock that has a
warning light on it for the times that it is submerged by the
tide and could become a danger to shipping. This small
rocky island is called the Lady Rock. Beyond it, on the
steamer's port side, is the Isle of Mull, rising away from the
low coastline to the heights of Ben More (3169 feet). By the
water's edge, perched on a craggy promontory, is Duart
Castle, seat of the Macleans of Duart, whose name derives
from the rock itself: Dubh Ard – the Black Height.

The castle dates back at least to the fourteenth century
and originally belonged to the Lords of the Isles who
granted it at the end of the fifteenth century to the

The Lady Rock (the small rock on the right).

Macleans, its owners today. It is a fascinating and evocative place, with its 63-foot-high keep and its dank dungeons. A walk round its interior on the days that its owner, Lord Maclean, opens it to the public is a memorable experience.

Not all the Macleans were as civilized as the present head of the clan, who is a member of the Queen's Household and a Knight of the Thistle.

One sixteenth-century chief, Lachlan Maclean, decided to rid himself of his wife. Realizing that he must do so in a way that would not arouse any suspicion among her kinsfolk who were the powerful Campbells of Argyll, he hit upon a clever scheme. The way to do it, Maclean persuaded himself, was to arrange his wife's death in such a way that it would look like an accident. As he sat in his castle pondering on how this could best be done, he watched the currents, sweeping up the Firth of Lorn between the Island of Mull and the mainland, gradually engulf a solitary rock a mile offshore.

That night, Lachlan Maclean overpowered his wife and tying her hands and feet, bundled her into a rowing boat drawn up on the shore. Ignoring her pleas for mercy he took her to the rock that was now above the tide mark and, quickly cutting through her bonds with his dirk, he left her kneeling at the water's edge. As he rowed away he thought he heard her cries die away and imagined that the tide had begun to do its work.

Next day, he was up at first light scanning the rock which was now showing above the water again as the tide ebbed. The rock was bare. Sitting at a table by a window overlooking the sea, Maclean began to pen a note to his wife's kinsmen expressing his concern at her disappearance and fearing the worst.

A few days later, he received a reply full of condolence and with an invitation to visit the Campbells at Inveraray Castle on Loch Fyne. Feeling rather pleased that his plot had worked so successfully, Maclean donned his widower's clothes and set off with a retinue of his men, to announce his wife's 'death' to her kinsmen.

At Inveraray, he received a warm welcome from all the Campbells assembled for the evening meal and he was escorted to the dining table at which many of the family were already sitting. Confused at coming into the crowded room after a hard day's riding, Lachlan Maclean did not pay particular attention to the lady sitting opposite him but, once settled, he raised his head to greet her again and discovered to his horror that he was looking into the eyes of his wife. The lady smiled but made no sign that she recognized him, nor did any of the others seated at the table act as if anything strange was happening. No one told him that a fisherman had rescued his wife from the rock and helped her make her way to Inveraray. The conversation continued along general lines and no mention was made of the reason for Maclean's visit. As the gruesome meal reached its end, the chief of the Campbells wished him good night and a pleasant stay but Maclean had had enough. With a muttered excuse about an important appointment on Mull, he left hurriedly, mounted his horse and rode off through the night as if the devil himself were after him.

He half expected to hear the sound of horses following him but there were none and as he neared the Firth of Lorn his spirits rose. Once on the island in his own stronghold, he felt even better and resolved to wipe the whole macabre episode from his mind. Having achieved this, Maclean began to live a normal life, journeying far afield – even as far as Edinburgh – on his business affairs. It was what the Campbells had been waiting for. Having lulled him into a false sense of security, a party of them led by Campbell of Cawdor, the wronged wife's brother, visited him one night in 1523 when he was sleeping at Edinburgh. Maclean woke to the sound of his door opening and as soon as he saw the faces illuminated by the light of the intruders' lantern, he knew his last moment had come. The Campbells went about their work quickly and quietly. No words were exchanged, for both victim and assassins understood the significance of the moment. When the murderers left, Maclean lay stretched out on his bed with his throat cut. Justice, in the manner of the times, had been done.

THE WALKS:	MAP SQUARE:
1. FROM THE A849 SOUTH OF CRAIGNURE TO DUART CASTLE.	1. Ordnance Survey Sheet 49/729338
2. FROM CRAIGNURE, VIA TOROSAY CASTLE, TO DUART CASTLE.	2. Ordnance Survey Sheet 49/718373

The walks are based on the assumption that you have left your car in Oban, and are travelling on the ferry or steamer. If you do have a car, you can choose for yourself the point at which you want to join them.

Mull is reached from Oban, which is a railhead and bus terminus. Caledonian MacBrayne ferries sail frequently to Craignure on Mull, passing the Lady Rock and Duart Castle, which can be seen on the port side.

To reach the start of the FIRST SUGGESTED WALK, take the 557 bus service from Craignure to Fionnphort (the ferry port for Iona) which passes near Duart. Ask for the Duart Castle stop (Lochdonhead). The walk starts at the beginning of the track from the A849 towards the headland. This is a pleasant walk, of about one and a half miles, past the hamlet of Kilpatrick and across undulating grassland to the point on which Duart stands.

The SECOND SUGGESTED WALK is a longer walk of about three and a half miles, starting from Craignure Pier, where you have come off the ferry. Follow the main road, the A849, south to the track leading off to the left about 400 yards past the inn at Craignure. This leads via a coastal walk of about a mile to Torosay Castle, a splendid Victorian baronial-style castle on the north-west side of Duart Bay. Part of the castle and its eleven acres of fine Italian terraced gardens are open to the public from May to mid-October, Monday to Friday, plus Sundays in July and August.

From Torosay Castle, rejoin the main road again for about a third of a mile before forking left along a minor road to Kilpatrick, Druimsoruaig and Duart Castle itself.

Despite its stern and forbidding exterior, Duart Castle, whose ruins were carefully restored early this century, is most attractive inside, with pleasantly furnished living rooms and a display featuring the work of the Boy Scouts, of which the present Lord Maclean was Chief Scout of the Commonwealth. The dungeons, complete with life-size models of prisoners once chained to the walls, provide a thrilling contrast, and a reminder of the more sombre side of the castle's history.

Duart Castle is open from May to September, Monday to Friday, plus Saturdays and Sunday afternoons in July and August.

28. THE *DUQUE DE FLORENCIA*
Tobermory

Tobermory is a very attractive, almost picture-book harbour town on the north-east side of the Isle of Mull. Its old houses are painted in bright pastel colours and on the quays where a few fishing boats and many pleasure craft are moored lies a picturesque tangle of nets, crab pots and other impedimenta. Along the front, which curves around the harbour, there are hotels of various grades, restaurants and delightful shops where you can buy tweed scarves, hats and sweaters as well as home-made jams and other delights.

The town stretches into the amphitheatre of hills that surround it and which protect the harbour from westerly gales. Its situation was the main reason for its development

Tobermory, Mull.

as a fishing port in the late eighteenth century. Long before this, however, the sheltered bay had provided refuge from storms for many ships. One of the most famous of these was a galleon from the ill-fated Spanish Armada which Philip II of Spain unleashed on England in 1588 in his efforts to seize the country in the name of Catholicism and of his deceased queen, Mary Tudor.

The story of how the huge fleet was dispersed by appalling weather and the resourcefulness and courage of sailors such as Effingham and Drake is well known and the tale of the disasters which overtook the remaining ships as they tried to get back to Spain by circumnavigating the British Isles has become legendary.

The galleon whose fate it was to end up sunk on the seabed in Tobermory Bay has never been identified, though several names have been suggested. A likely candidate is the *Duque de Florencia*, one of the ships that managed to round Cape Wrath and head south. Beset by storms and in urgent need of repairs, her captain decided to put into Tobermory Bay.

As it happened, at the time the galleon put into the harbour two branches of the MacLean clan were involved in a bitter feud. MacLean of Duart, the chief of one of the factions, went aboard the Spanish ship and finding that it was carrying soldiers, conceived a scheme whereby he could score off the MacLeans of Coll. Having learnt that the captain was short of provisions, he agreed to supply these in return for the loan of a hundred Spanish soldiers and a cash payment. The captain could hardly refuse the offer, for his situation was desperate, and he knew that if he did not feed his men he might well have a mutiny on his hands. The agreement made, MacLean now ordered his men to put food aboard the ship while he and the force of Spaniards now at his command set sail in small boats for Mingary Castle on the Ardnamurchan shore. Carried away by his success, MacLean also attacked his hated kinsmen's possessions on the nearby islands of Eigg, Rum, Canna and Muck.

When he returned, the Spanish galleon had been fully provisioned and was ready to take to sea but no payment for the services rendered had been offered. MacLean reminded the captain of their bargain but received no satisfaction. Realizing that guile would have more chance of success than a confrontation with the Spaniards who had already shown their fighting ability against the MacLeans of Coll, the chief of the Duart MacLeans had the soldiers escorted back to the ship under the command of one of his most trusted lieutenants, thought to have been Donald Glas MacLean. The captain of the *Duque de Florencia* promptly took him hostage.

That night, the people of Mull were awoken by a tremendous explosion. Running out on to the water's edge they saw the *Duque de Florencia* engulfed in flames and sinking fast as she tried to sail out into the Sound of Mull.

To this day nobody knows what went wrong. Had MacLean's lieutenant set fire to the ship to free himself and miscalculated the extent of the blaze so that it reached the powder magazine? It had been rumoured that the ship was loaded with treasure. Had her captain, therefore, blown her up rather than have his valuable cargo fall into MacLean's hands?

Only three of the crew survived the disaster and they could give no explanation. Many attempts have been made to salvage the wreck and to discover the reason for the unexpected end to the story of the *Duque de Florencia* but to this day no one has succeeded. Various bits and pieces from the wreck have been found, including guns and shot, and some silver plate, but every year the possibility of solving this mystery of the sea becomes more distant as the ship sinks further and further into the clay bed which is its last resting place.

THE WALK:
FROM TOBERMORY PIER
TO LOCHAN A GHURRA-
BAIN, AND BACK.

MAP SQUARE:
Ordnance Survey Sheet
47/506553
A pleasant 3 mile stroll
around Tobermory Bay.

Tobermory, whose name is an anglicization of the Gaelic for St Mary's Well, is the chief town of Mull, and an immensely popular place in summer. Accommodation is usually heavily booked, except in the off-season, for the town has a fine reputation which is well deserved.

Tobermory is on the east coast of Mull, at the island's northern end, and is on the A848 coast road from the ferry port at Craignure. From Tobermory, the round-the-island road continues as the B8073. There is also a minor road from Tobermory that goes north into the delightfully named, though rather bleak, area of Mishnish.

Our walk in Tobermory starts at the pier on the northern side of the bay. The Duque de Florencia *is thought to be sunk in the bay not far from the pier, but as she is buried in thirty feet of clay, eleven fathoms down, there is nothing of her for you to see.*

From the pier, walk around the harbour, with the beach below you and Tobermory's main street beside you. Many of the houses date from the eighteenth century and have delightful pointed attics. The ground floors of many of them house shops, banks, Scottish woollen shops and the town's Information Centre. The harbour itself is a splendid picture, full of pleasure boats and a few fishing craft, with seagulls crying overhead and the hills around fringed with trees.

A few yards past the Information Centre, near the southern end of the village, a path strikes off from the A848 along the shore of the bay. Along here, you will obtain some enchanting, and very photographable, views of Tobermory and the bay.

The walk is wooded all the way along the shore. At the southern end of the harbour, it follows a slight incline up the

Lochan a Ghurrabain. Here, the view east is dominated by Calve Island, whose protection ensures Tobermory Bay its unruffled calm.

From pier to loch is barely one and a half miles, so if you wish to extend your walk, rather than returning directly to Tobermory, you can follow the path beyond the lochan, which emerges on to the A848 about three-quarters of a mile south of the lochan. From here, the walk back along the A848 to Tobermory pier is just over three miles.

29. THE HUNCHBACKS OF IONA
Iona

The island of Iona is one of those places that seem destined to be spiritual focus points of the world. Whether it is because of the events that occur in them or whether their situation is such that they attract these happenings, is a matter for argument, but there is no doubt about their effect on the visitor. On Iona, one is immediately overcome by a sense of presence. It is not only the beauty of its setting, or its cliffs and sandy beaches, but also the feeling – similar to the one you get in old houses – that the spirit of the people who lived on it are somehow still there in the rocks and the heather and in the breeze that sweeps in from the Atlantic.

Iona was known to the Norsemen long before St Columba arrived from Ireland in AD 563 to found his monastery but where the seafarers left no trace of their visits, St Columba and his companions left many. Far more than mere passing marauders, they landed on Iona with the intention of using it as a base for their missionary work on the mainland.

In the Dark Ages, monks were the guardians of culture, and as Iona's monastery developed so its library became filled with manuscripts handwritten and decorated by the monks. The monastery's fame and the success of the Iona monks in converting the heathen chiefs of the mainland to Christianity, soon made Iona a place in which the Scottish kings were traditionally buried and before they had ceased to be a ruling line in Scotland some forty-eight of them had been buried there. Among the tombs (now disappeared) were those of Duncan, and of his murderer, Macbeth.

Rebuilt several times in the course of its history, the

Cathedral of Iona was just a ruin at the end of the last century. The building that one sees today is largely a modern reconstruction. Many of the restorations, such as the monastic buildings and the cloister, were rebuilt as recently as the 1930s. This recent work in no way detracts from the atmosphere and dignity of the monastery, for it has been built upon the original plan and its square grey tower evokes perfectly the fortress-like style of early church buildings which were designed for defensive as well as spiritual ends.

Iona Cathedral.

Though Iona's fame rests on its Christian history, the island also has its pagan spirits who, once upon a time, were not averse to playing nasty practical jokes as well as doing people favours. One legend that recalls the arbitrary behaviour of the spirits of the faery world that exists all over Scotland recounts the story of a certain Fachie, a young man who had the misfortune to be born with a hunchback. Though burdened with this cruel deformity, young Fachie was a good-humoured lad and eager to be helpful to everyone. Since the other young people in their thoughtless way made fun of him Fachie used often to wander off up the 300-foot hill which you will see today lying behind the cathedral. He would sit at the summit looking out over the magnificent view of thirty or more islands that were visible all over the sea.

One day, while he was sitting lost in contemplation, he heard a voice singing, or rather beginning, a song because the words never got beyond a phrase which ran 'Monday, Tuesday . . .' His attention having been caught by the repetitious song which never got going, Fachie looked round for the owner of the voice and saw him behind a nearby rock. He was a very small faery man who danced around as he hummed his tune and then, arriving at the word 'Tuesday', would stamp on the ground and screw his face up into a grimace of anger and frustration.

Fachie looked at him as he started his song and dance again and this time as the little man said 'Tuesday' and stammered once more to a halt, Fachie shouted 'Wednesday!' The little man looked up in surprise and then the incipient frown on his face turned into a smile and, raising his knee, he stamped gleefully on the ground and carried on dancing.

After repeating the song several times, and being helped over his stumbling block by Fachie, the little man at last mastered the word that had been impeding his enjoyment.

When Fachie got home that night and looked at himself in the mirror he was surprised to find that instead of the hunched youth he was accustomed to seeing, there stood before him a straight, slim young man whom he would hardly have recognized except that he had his own face. When he had recovered from the shock, Fachie danced with joy and ran out to tell everyone about his strange experience.

News of the miracle spread to the island of Tiree where Hugh, who was also a hunchback, heard about it. Immediately, Hugh set about getting a boat to sail to Iona so that the little man could cure him also. He climbed to the top of the hill and waited and, just as he had hoped, he heard the sound of a voice singing 'Monday, Tuesday, Wednesday'. Looking out from his hiding place, Hugh saw the little man leaping up and down and when he had reached the word 'Wednesday' Hugh shouted 'Thursday' in a loud voice. This so surprised the little dancer that he fell over on his back which made Hugh burst out in guffaws of laughter. The little man was so upset at the sound of the laughter that he picked himself up and without even bothering to dust his clothes ran off through the heather. Hugh continued to shout with laughter and to demand that the little man come back and cure his hump for having taught him another day of the week. The little man had disappeared however and the only sound that Hugh could hear was the sighing of the wind through the grass. 'Oh, well,' he thought, 'it will all be sorted out when I get home, I expect.'

But when he got home and looked in the mirror he discovered that not only had the faery not done anything about his hump but he had given him Fachie's as well. Hugh was furious and cursed the little faery man roundly but it did no good and he never understood why the little man had not repaid the favour he had done him in the same way as he had repaid Fachie's.

THE WALK:
ROUND IONA, STARTING
AT THE MONASTERY.

MAP SQUARE:
Ordnance Survey Sheet
48/286245
A tour, rather than a walk, round this tiny island, with no specific route suggested.

The route to Iona is via Oban, from where you take the passenger and car ferry to Craignure on Mull. As the ferry approaches Mull you can see the Lady Rock and Duart Castle, scenes of the attempted murder of Lady Duart by her husband (see p. 170). From Craignure, the A849 crosses Mull to Fionnphort, from where there is a ferry to Iona.

Alternatively, there are frequent steamer excursions in summer from Oban direct to Iona. The route for these is south through the Sound of Kerrera and then along the Mull coast, past the old and new Maclean castles at the entrance to Loch Buie. Further on, the coast becomes more rocky with basalt rocks forming columns at Carsaig Arches similar to those on Staffa; stone for Iona Cathedral was quarried along this coast. At Nun's Cave there are carvings thought to have inspired the designs on the Iona Crosses.

After passing through the reefs known as the Torrins, the steamer arrives at Iona, which is a tiny island only three miles long and half a mile wide. Sir Hugh Fraser bought the island in 1979 and presented it to the National Trust for Scotland, and visitors may walk freely over its low hills and round its bays. Because of Iona's size, and because places of interest are scattered about, we are not suggesting a specific walk here: discover its beauties in your own time!

Centre of interest on Iona is the monastery and the cathedral. The monastery was destroyed and rebuilt many times. Just south of it, the cathedral was begun in the twelfth century and it, too, was reduced to ruins. Most of the work of restoration has been carried out in this century, much of it by the Iona Community who live and work here.

The oldest surviving building on Iona is St Oran's Chapel which was probably built in the later eleventh century by St Margaret. Other points of interest include the remains of the thirteenth-century nunnery and the 14-foot-high St Martin's Cross, dating from the ninth or tenth centuries, which stood opposite the west door of the cathedral. Carvings on the Cross depict the Holy Family, Daniel in the lions' den *and other biblical scenes.*

Behind the cathedral rises a 332-foot hill, Dun-I (the 'island fortress'), from the summit of which views over the island and the surrounding sea can be enjoyed. If the weather is clear, you should be able to count thirty islands.

If the steamer's timetable allows it, try to fit in a walk to the south of the island, to Port-na-Curaich ('the port of the coracle') where St Columba and his followers are traditionally said to have landed. The Spouting Cave, on the west coast south of the golf course, is also worth a visit.

ALSO AVAILABLE IN THE WALKS AND LEGENDS
SERIES PUBLISHED BY GRANADA PAPERBACKS

LAKELAND WALKS AND LEGENDS
by Brian J Bailey   £1.50

LONDON WALKS AND LEGENDS
by Mary Cathcart Borer   £1.25

WEST COUNTRY WALKS AND LEGENDS
by J H N Mason   £1.25

WELSH WALKS AND LEGENDS
by Showell Styles   £1.00

SCOTTISH WALKS AND LEGENDS VOLUME 2
by Janice Anderson and Edmund Swinglehurst   £1.50

*All these books are available at your local bookshop or newsagent, or can be
ordered direct from the publisher. Just tick the titles you want and fill in the
form below.*

Name ....

Address ....

....

Write to Granada Cash Sales, PO Box 11, Falmouth, Cornwall TR10 9EN

Please enclose remittance to the value of the cover price plus:

UK: 40p for the first book, 18p for the second book plus 13p per copy for
each additional book ordered to a maximum charge of £1.49.

BFPO and EIRE: 40p for the first book, 18p for the second book plus 13p
per copy for the next 7 books, thereafter 7p per book.

OVERSEAS: 60p for the first book and 18p for each additional book.

*Granada Publishing reserve the right to show new retail prices on covers, which
may differ from those previously advertised in the text or elsewhere.*